EDML

C000133977

TRAVELS

IN

THE WESTERN CAUCASUS,

INCLUDING A TOUR THROUGH

**IMERETIA, MINGRELIA, TURKEY, MOLDAVIA, GALICIA,
SILESIA, AND MORAVIA,
IN 1836**

In Two Volumes

Volume 1

Elibron Classics
www.elibron.com

TRAVELS

IN

THE WESTERN CAUCASUS,

&c. &c.

IN TWO VOLUMES.

VOL. I.

T. C. Savill, Printer, 107, St. Martin's Lane, Charing Cross.

Drawn & Engraved by J. Tucker.

GUERILLA WARFARE IN THE CAUCASUS.

Published by Henry Colburn, Great North rough Street 1838.

TRAVELS

IN THE

WESTERN CAUCASUS,

INCLUDING A TOUR THROUGH

IMERITIA, MINGRELIA, TURKEY, MOLDAVIA, GALICIA,
SILESIA, AND MORAVIA,
IN 1836.

By EDMUND SPENCER, Esq.

Author of " Travels in Circassia," &c.

BIVOUAC IN THE CAUCASUS.

VOL. I.

LONDON:
HENRY COLBURN, GREAT MARLBOROUGH STREET.
1838.

PREFACE.

WHEN all eyes were turned towards the East, —when an active demonstration of the smothered dislike of Russia towards England had burst forth in the capture of a British merchant vessel,— when the subject of the war in the Caucasus, and the right of Russia to its sovereignty, founded upon the treaty of Adrianople, occupied the public mind, I felt it my duty to my country, and to the general interests of humanity, to hasten the publication of my travels in Circassia, in order to assist in laying open to the world the ambitious plans of Russia, her unjust invasion of the Caucasus, and various other facts connected with the same subject. This obliged me to abridge many details, and terminate my narrative somewhat abruptly. The present work is therefore a continuation of the former, and supplies several omissions necessary to illustrate the character of the war, together with the manners and customs of the inhabitants of the WESTERN CAUCASUS. It also contains an account of my tour homeward, through some of the most interesting countries on the Black Sea, to Constantinople, and from thence through Bulgaria, Moldavia, Galicia, &c., to Vienna.

I cannot take leave of the principal subject of my work—THE WESTERN CAUCASUS—without expressing a hope, however little I may indulge the expectation, that some attempt may be made by the English government to avert the cruel destiny now impending over the inhabitants of that unfortunate country. Before the hues of Autumn shall tint the foliage of the forest, Russia will have made one of the most determined—one of the most gigantic—efforts to crush the independence of the Caucasus ever perpetrated by selfish aggrandizing ambition,—black and lengthened as may be the catalogue of its atrocities.

An overwhelming army, supplied with all that

can give force to its operations, and the equally
dangerous artillery of political intrigue and
bribery, are engines which, when directed with
the talent that Russia has ever displayed in gaining any object she may have had in view, excite
the apprehension that the untutored bravery of
a handful of mountaineers will avail but little
against so effective a combination. But will
England, will Europe, have nothing to answer for
to posterity, in permitting the fall of Circassia?
Are our councils to be for ever swayed by that
timid policy which provides but for the present,
regardless of the future? The interests of our
children demand another line of action—demand
that we should dam up the stream before it swells
into a torrent. Why, then, not do it? Why
allow Russia to proceed unchecked, unmolested
in the career of ambition she has marked out for
herself? Russia, however, ought to remember,
that although she may calculate upon the support
of a few despotic rulers, the intelligent mind
of Europe is opposed to her, and that she is
regarded as the common enemy of liberty and

knowledge :—these, we confidently anticipate, will ultimately control and coerce her ; and if we are to judge from present appearances, it must be some irresistible manifestation of public opinion which shall effect this, and not, we fear, the spirited remonstrances of the present rulers of Europe. For instance, although they are aware that Circassia is an independent country, and was independent of Turkey prior to the treaty of Adrianople, which of them would dare to insist that Russia should terminate the barbarous hostilities she is now carrying on against that country, or aid the mountaineers in their unequal struggle, notwithstanding every inch of territory gained by her is in direct opposition to the best interests of Europe? We fear this brave people will have no other help, save that of Heaven and " their own good swords."

I cannot conclude my preface without performing an act of justice, however tardy, towards the literary fame of Miss Head, the accomplished translator of Klopstock's celebrated poem, the " Messiah." I allude to a passage in my work on Germany, wherein I severely censured the English translation, by which I meant the prose version, being ignorant, at the time, of the verse translation by that lady, in which she has not only done every justice to the admirable original, but added a new gem to our own literature. I should have made the *amende honorable* in the second edition of my work on Germany, if I had not been absent from England at the time of its publication.

E. S.

London,—May, 1838.

ILLUSTRATIONS.

VOL. I.

VOL. II.

CONTENTS

OF

THE FIRST VOLUME.

CHAPTER I.

CHAPTER II.

CHAPTER III.

CHAPTER IV.

CHAPTER V.

CHAPTER XVIII.

CHAPTER XIX.

CHAPTER XX.

CHAPTER XXVIII.

CHAPTER XXIX.

TRAVELS

IN THE

WESTERN CAUCASUS,

&c. &c.

CHAPTER I.

Introductory remarks — Observations on the Caucasian
isthmus—Its inhabitants—The Attéghéi, or Circassian
tribes—Their origin—Error of modern writers in con-
founding them with the Tartars of Koumania—Identity
of the Koumanian Tartars and the inhabitants of Upper
and Lower Koumani in Hungary.

In this uncertain world, where the promise of
to-day is so often of necessity broken by the event
of to-morrow, it gives me great pleasure that I
am afforded an opportunity of redeeming the
pledge I made in my last work to continue the
narrative of my travels ; and, as I am no longer
on the wing, passing rapidly from scene to scene,
from country to country, exposed alternately to

disease and danger, or liable, when taking notes, to be seized as a spy or a sorcerer by the inhabitants of the half-civilized countries I explored, I hope to be able to render my pages more worthy the perusal of my readers.

In consequence of the increasing interest attached to the Caucasian provinces on the Black Sea, I am particularly desirous of contributing every possible information respecting them, more especially as the heroism of their inhabitants has already excited the sympathy of the whole civilized world,—a people who, although feeble in numerical force, have, unaided by any other power, successfully maintained their independence, notwithstanding the mighty efforts which have been continued with little intermission for the last fifty years, by their formidable neighbour, Russia, to subdue them.   I shall therefore, without further introduction, proceed with my observations on the Western Caucasus and its inhabitants.   It may, however, be advisable to inform those among my readers who have not perused my preceding work on Circassia, that a combination of favourable circumstances attended my visit to that interesting and almost unknown country.

An invitation from Count Worenzow, Governor

General of South Russia, to accompany him on
his voyage round the Black Sea, and visit the
Russian settlements in Circassia, Mingrelia, and
Gourial, was the means of procuring me a variety
of information respecting the political situation of
countries which had been hitherto, owing to Russian influence, hermetically sealed from the in-
spection of a foreigner.

Again, when I visited the interior of Circassia,
I was favoured with introductions from some of
the principal effendis of the Turkish empire to
several chiefs and elders of the tribes, which insured me a hospitable reception. For a detailed
account of these tours, I beg leave to refer my
readers to my former volumes, these being, in
fact, a continuation of the same work.

The Caucasian isthmus, with its stupendous
mountains and snow-clad alps, forming the natural barrier between two great sections of the
globe, Asia and Europe, is, if not the most remarkable, the most imperfectly known of any
region of the ancient world; indeed, nearly the
whole of the geographical knowledge we possess
respecting the interior is, for the most part, erroneous, consequent on the inaccessible nature of
the country, and the great danger of journeying

through it. Here the traveller is exposed, not
only to the bullet of the Russian invader, the predatory horde, but to the probability of having to
endure perpetual slavery; hence we cannot wonder that the stranger has rarely found his way into
a country where, though he might advance the
purposes of science or the diffusion of knowledge,
he might also sacrifice his liberty, or his life. An
additional obstacle to obtaining accurate information arises from the circumstance that nearly each
tribe who inhabits it speaks a different dialect.

Those travellers who have hitherto written on
the Caucasus have been principally Russian agents;
consequently, being aware of the political views
of that power, we cannot depend on their statements when describing its strength, resources,
and political situation, the policy of Russia, since
the first attempt of Peter to bring it under subjection, having invariably been to throw a veil
over the actual state of that country.

Besides, that part of the isthmus denominated
the Western Caucasus, and to which my excursions were principally confined, has ever been,
owing to the bravery of its inhabitants, a sealed
land to Russian encroachments, with the exception of a few forts on the coast of the Black Sea;

we cannot, therefore, feel surprised that not one of her delegated chroniclers of Circassia has ever penetrated into the interior of the country. The whole of the statements of Güldenstadt, Reineggs, Pallas, and Klaproth, having been derived from the information of ignorant Russian prisoners, Armenian pedlars, or Karaite Jews, and not from personal observation.

As several of my critical contemporaries have counselled me to communicate such information as I may be possessed of relative to the history of the origin of the inhabitants of the Caucasus, and the commercial advantages that country offers to Great Britain, it may be as well to enter into a few of these details previously to commencing the account of my journey homewards.

The Western Caucasus, comprehending the whole of the immense district, (extending from the Kouban to Mingrelia, from the Russian military road Wladikawkas, or Terkkalla,) which, commencing at the middle Kouban, and running along the snowy mountains, terminates in Georgia, is inhabited by various tribes, who, however differing in origin and language, are governed by princes, elders, and nobles, that claim one com-

mon descent, and are distinguished by the name
of Attéghéi. The inhabitants of the two Kabardahs, and several of the tribes who reside on the
coast of the Black Sea, from the Kouban to
Upper Abasia, speak the Circassian language
with the purest accent, and are considered to be
of genuine Attéghéi lineage. To this people also
belongs the distinction of being more brave and
civilized, more hospitable and courteous to their
guests, more stubbornly tenacious of their independence, and uncompromising in their enmity
to Russia, than any other.

Attéghéi, the name by which these people distinguish themselves, is, however, not that by which
they are known to their neighbours, as I have
already shewn in my preceding work on Circassia.
From their own appellation, Attéghéi, signifying a
people inhabiting a country between two seas, we
may, with a great degree of probability, infer
them to have been the original inhabitants. This
supposition is not, however, encouraged by the
traditions of the Circassians themselves, nor by
the details given to us by the Tartar and Russian
historians. The latter nation possesses several
highly curious and valuable works on the history,
origin, manners, and customs of the various in-

habitants of the vast countries over which she
now exercises sovereign sway ; but, unfortunately
for the diffusion of knowledge, they are hermetically sealed, except to the perusal of a privi-
leged few. During my voyage round the Black
Sea, that excellent nobleman, Count Worenzow,
supplied me with a variety of interesting works
on the Caucasus, from which, and I may add
from his own intelligent remarks respecting the
origin of its inhabitants, I have compiled a few
notes, which I hope may be found worthy the
perusal of the reader, more particularly as the
Caucasian race has occupied the attention of the
learned of every age and country. I would also
endeavour to rectify the opinions so currently received, founded upon the statements of modern
travellers in the Caucasus, some of whom contend that the Attéghéi tribes are the descendants
of the Koumanian Tartars, while others, with
equal confidence, maintain them to be sprung
from a colony of wandering Arabs.

With regard to the first statement, it appears
that, previous to the conquests of Genghis-Khan,
an extremely powerful people, called by the Russian historians Polowzians, occupied the whole of
the extensive countries between the Wolga and

the Don; they are mentioned for the first time in
Russian history about the middle of the tenth
century. From this period till their final disper-
sion by Tuschi-Khan, son of Genghis-Khan, in
1225, they carried on the most incessant and active warfare against Russia, burning the villages
and ravaging the country on to the very gates of
Moscow. The Russians having been compelled,
about the same epoch, to submit to the Mongul
yoke, no further mention is made of them in history.

From the identity of the Polowzians of the
Russian chronicles with the Koumanians of the
Byzantines, it has been conjectured, from the
similarity of the names found in history belonging to that people and those of the Attéghéi tribes
of the Caucasus, that they are a remnant of the
Koumanian Tartars; but modern research con-
futes this opinion, it being now ascertained that
the Polowzians or Koumanians were nothing more
than subjects of Circassian princes, whose names
alone have been recorded in history; their territories, called Kabari, (Kabardah,) according to a
singularly curious manuscript map found in the
imperial library at Vienna, joined the country of
the Koumanians, over whom, in all probability,

the Kabardian princes exercised some sort of nominal sovereignty.

No historian, however, particularizes the chiefs of Koumani or their country; they merely record the bravery of the princes, and the beauty of their daughters, who, they say, were sought in marriage by the kings of Hungary, the Byzantine princes, and the Czars of Muscovy, an honour which would not have been conferred upon them were they a Tartar race, proverbially deficient in personal charms, and despised by their European neighbours. As to the fact of the Koumanians being a Tartar horde, no doubt whatever exists, that having been fully proved by several historians and eminent travellers, particularly Ruysbrock the monk, who visited their country in the early part of the thirteenth century: he says, when travelling over the vast steppe of Western Tartary, "This whole plain was, previously to the irruption of the Mongul Tartars, inhabited by the Koumanians, who called themselves Kapschat Tartars, and were descended from a great chief of that name, and traced their origin from Ishmael."

De Plano Carpini, who was sent by Pope Innocent IV. to Tartary, previous to the visit of Ruysbrock, corroborates this statement, asserting that the Koumani and Polowtzi were one people, and of Tartar origin. *Cumani id est Polowtzi ex deserto egressi.* Anna Comnena says, that the Patzinakes (Petscheneges) spoke the same language as the Koumani, were of the same Tartar origin, and claimed kindred with the Turks, Torkmeni, &c.

It has been asserted, and generally believed, that the Koumanians and Petscheneges, who were also denominated Kangars, on being driven by the Monguls from their settlements in Western Tartary, established themselves in Hungary, the former having given their name to a district in that country called Great and Little Koumani: now if the Hungarian Koumani and the Attéghéi tribes in Circassia were sprung from one common origin, should we not be able to trace it in their persons, customs, and especially language? but so far from this being the case, no one of these particulars tends to establish any such identity of descent, the Circassian language being unlike every other with which modern philologists are familiar; for although the Koumanian language is extinct in Hungary, manuscripts have been preserved which incontestibly prove it to have been a Tartar-Turkish dialect, not only in words but in grammatical construction.

CHAPTER II.

Refutation of the opinion that the Circassians are of Arab descent—Mamelukes of Egypt—Arab-chan the supposed progenitor of the Circassians — His history—Ineffectual attempts of Russia to explore the Western Caucasus—Ossetinian tribes—Their Median origin—Opinions of Pallas respecting the Circassians and the Krim-Tartars—Unquestionable proofs of the rule of the Circassians in the Crimea—Opinions of the ancient writers respecting the Circassians—Cossacks of the Don and the Kouban not of Muscovite extraction.

HAVING shewn in my preceding chapter that the Attéghéi tribes of the Caucasus are not of Tartar origin, we shall now proceed to the consideration of their reported Arab descent. According to Pallas and other modern writers, to which may be added the traditions still preserved in the families of some of the Kabardian chiefs, the princes of Circassia deduce their pedigree from Inal, a celebrated chieftain that flourished in the

fifteenth century, and left his patrimony to be
divided among his five sons ; this chief was said
to be descended from Arab-Chan, a famous
Arabian prince, who settled with a small retinue
between the Kouban and Anapa on the Black
Sea.

This was currently believed till a more intimate
acquaintance with the traditions of the Circassians, together with a more correct knowledge of
the history of the Arabs during the sovereignty
of the Circassian Mameluke dynasty in Egypt,
proved the contrary. This power established
itself in that country after the extinction of the
Egyptian Sultans in 1300, and maintained its
ascendancy till 1517, when their chief, Tuman
Bey, was taken prisoner by the Turkish Sultan
Selim I.

Among these Mameluke rulers we find, in
1453, one who bore the name of Inal, and it
appears was not the son, but the relative, of
Arab-Chan. This chief, instead of being of
Arabian descent, was in reality a Mameluke.
Khan of a powerful tribe of Arabs, and known
in history as Arab-Chan, from the bravery of
himself and followers, his influence became so
formidable that he made an attempt to seize

the reins of sovereign authority, and rule all
Egypt; but not succeeding, he was compelled to
fly, and escaped with his principal adherents to
the country of his ancestors, where, having
formed a settlement, between the Kouban and
Anapa, on the Black Sea, he built a large town;
the site is still pointed out, on the banks of the
Nefil, and seems to have been regularly fortified
with ramparts, moat, and several forts, which
now appear like small hills descending to the
marshes of the river Kouban.

It is highly probable that this Arab-Chan,
from his known bravery and ambitious disposition, established a species of sovereign authority over his countrymen; and having left a son
called Inal, his descendants were proud to
acknowledge so renowned a chieftain as their
progenitor. On the other hand, if the princes
of Circassia derived their origin from an Arab so
late as the sixteenth century, they would still
retain some portion of the Arabian language.
This, in fact, was, until very recently, supposed
to be the case, from the circumstance of the
chiefs and nobles speaking an entirely different
language from the people; but, so far from
resembling the Arabic, it bears, like that of the

common dialect of the Circassians, no affinity to
any other now known.

The Russian Government, with a laudable zeal
to promote the purposes of science, and to
diffuse a more correct knowledge of the country
and inhabitants of the Caucasus, and, no doubt,
to advance its own political views, annually
equips and sends forth intelligent and well-
informed travellers, at its own expense. In consequence, however, of the implacable hatred
entertained by the Attéghéi tribes of the Western
Caucasus towards their ancient foe, and the inaccessible nature of the country, its efforts have
been hitherto abortive, either in endeavouring to
establish friendly intercourse with the natives, or
in procuring a favourable reception for any of
its delegated agents, who have not been able to
penetrate beyond the line of her forts established
on the Wladikaukas, or on the coast of the
Black Sea; and now, since the war has assumed
a more sanguinary character, it is too certain
that this country will long remain unexplored.
Since the partial subjugation of the Ossetinians,
(previously supposed to be a tribe of Tartars,) inhabiting that part of the north-eastern Caucasus
over which Russia has conducted her military

road to Georgia, and which has led to a more intimate acquaintance with the language, customs, and manners of that people, it has been conjectured with great probability that they are descended from the ancient Medes ; this has been deduced from their language, which is a dialect of the Median, and, being intermingled with a few Sarmatian words, — such as Don, signifying a river, or water,—it is presumed, from various data, as well as from the traditions of the Ossetinians themselves, that they are the offspring of a Median colony, which Diodorus Siculus relates as having been conducted by the Scythians to that part of the ancient Sarmatia watered by the Don.* This statement was subsequently confirmed by Pliny, when describing the banks of the Don.

With respect, however, to the Circassians, notwithstanding all that has been written on the subject, their origin still remains veiled in obscurity. That they were at one time a powerful people, and their language spread not only over the Caucasian isthmus and the Crimea, but

---

* The appellations of the great rivers in the eastern part of Europe are all of Sarmatian origin ; for instance, the Don, Donau, (Danube,) Donaster, (Dniester,) Donapris, (Dnieper.)

along the banks of the Kouban and the Don, is proved by a reference to the Greek historians. This is further established by the circumstance That several towns, rivers, and districts still retain their Circassian appellations. Pallas, who long resided in the Crimea, and was well acquainted with its history and geography, expressed in the latter part of his life the opinion that the Circassians were the original inhabitants of that peninsula; and from the resemblance of the Krim Tartars to that people, he infers them to be a remnant, whose language and customs, in process of time, became merged in those of their conquerors. Be this as it may, an immense castle, now in ruins, still preserves its Circassian name; as does also the vast steppe between the rivers Belbik and Katscha.

The ancients, particularly the Byzantines, always denominated the inhabitants of the Western Caucasus, Zychians, the Greek word for Circassians, and describe their settlements to have extended from Pitzounda, the ancient Pythus, along the shores of the Black Sea, to the mouth of the Kouban, being the precise territory they now occupy, and to which Russia has laid claim.

Signor Interiani, a Genoese, who visited the Caucasus in the early part of the sixteenth century, tells us, in his account of the Circassians, that they inhabited the whole coast of the Black Sea, from the Don to the Cimmerian Bosphorus, and from thence to the mouth of the Kouban, along the sea coast to the Phase in Mingrelia, a coast upwards of five hundred miles in extent, while their territory inland was, in many places, sufficiently broad to occupy the traveller eight days in journeying across it. He further states, that their language differed entirely from any spoken by the neighbouring nations, and that the men were distinguished for their hospitality, bravery, and predatory habits, and the women for their industrious habits and great beauty.

For the fact that the Circassians were also known by the name of Kassack, (Cossack,) we may refer to several writers of unquestionable veracity, a name by which they are still known to some of their neighbours. Constantine Torphyrogenneta, who in 948 wrote an account of these countries and their inhabitants in the neighbourhood of the Black Sea, places the province of Kassachia* beyond the Kouban, near Mount Caucasus, and terms the inhabitants Kassack-

* There is still a district in the Western Caucasus known by the name of the Alti-Kassack.

Zychians (Cossack Circassians.)   Ibn el Vardi, the famous Arabian geographer of the twelfth century, when alluding to the inhabitants of the Western Caucasus, also appears to identify Kassachia with Circassia by his character of the personal charms of the women, for, in the exaggerated style of eastern phraseology, he exclaims, " Praised be Allah for creating mortals so infinitely beautiful and perfect."

Wolomerewick, one of the earliest princes of Muscovy mentioned in Russian history, having conquered the Isle of Taman, near the sea of Azow, its prince assumed the title of Sovereign Lord of Kassachia.   It is also worth notice, that the original denomination given by the Russians to the Cossacks was Tcherkessians (Circassians.) But whether the Cossacks of the present day are sprung from the same stock as the Circassians remains an historical problem not yet satisfactorily proved, either by their own traditions or by the accounts of any historian.   The word Kassach is equally obscure when applied to the Circassians, for although Kassack in Tartar, Turkish, and Russian, means a hired soldier, it is foreign to these languages.   Perhaps the Circassians, who it appears in every age led a sort of roving half military, half bandit life, and were at one time the life guards of the Sultans of Egypt and Turkey and of the Khans of the Krimea, were known to the surrounding nations by that appellation, who gave it to every tribe that led a similar life.

This much, however, is certain, that the Cossacks of the Don and the Kouban, notwithstanding they speak the Russian language, are not of Russian extraction, as their features are handsomer and more expressive, and their forms exhibit a symmetry and elegance but little inferior to their neighbours the Circassians. They are also distinguished, like the mountaineers, by a love of freedom and independence, which they evince by adhering to their ancient institutions; hence, strictly speaking, the country of the Cossacks cannot be called a Russian province, as the inhabitants retain their own laws, and elect their own Ataman, at the same time acknowledging the supremacy of Russia.

The Cossacks also possess the same acuteness, quickness of apprehension, and shrewdness, that generally distinguish the Asiatics. It must however be confessed, that they too much resemble the Sclavonians in their love for intoxicating liquors.

CHAPTER III.

Great and Little Kabardah, the original country of the Circassians—The Amazons and the Scythians on the banks of the Tanais—Tradition of the Circassians respecting the Amazons—Singular coincidence between their traditions and the history of the Amazons by Herodotus—Origin of the Sarmatians—Opinions of the ancient writers on that subject.

BUT to return to the Circassians and their genealogy. Great and Little Kabardah are considered to be that part of the Caucasus in which the Circassian language is spoken by prince, noble, and peasant, in its greatest purity; and as the inhabitants are distinguished by the usual characteristics of the Attéghéi tribes, the men for a certain haughty martial air, expressive features, great physical strength, height of stature, and symmetry of form, and the women by their personal attractions,—from these circumstances,

and also that history makes no mention of the
Caucasus being overrun by predatory hordes,
or that the mountaineers at any time submitted
to a foreign yoke, we may assume that the two
Kabardahs have been occupied from time immemorial by the same people. If so, we have another proof, from the similarity of names and
places in the Kabardahs and the Krimea, that
both countries were originally inhabited by the
same race; or that the peninsula, at some epoch
or other, was ruled by Kabardian princes. It is,
however, a singular fact, that the history and
origin of a great people, who evidently ruled
over, or inhabited, a vast tract of country, extending from the Caspian Sea to the Don, should
present no stronger claims to authenticity than
the songs of bards, the traditions of poets, and
the names of districts, places, and rivers, while
almost every other nation, however barbarous, possesses some historical records upon which we can
depend, some account of its connexion with the
people that preceded it.

In order to arrive at anything like a satisfactory conclusion respecting the origin of this singular people, we must refer to the history of the
Amazons, and to that of their conquerors, the

equestrian tribe of Scythian youth, and assume
them to be the progenitors of the Circassian
people.   This supposition carries with it a strong
probability of truth, from the fact that several
writers of antiquity on the history of the Amazons—for instance, Metrodotus, Skassius, Strabo,
and particularly Theophanes, who accompanied
Pompey in his expedition to Albania, and was
well acquainted with the country,—have by common consent agreed, that a band of warlike
women inhabited that part of the Caucasus now
known as Kabardah, and the plains watered by
the Kuma and the Therek, the ancient Merma-
dalis, a statement still preserved in the traditions
of various tribes in the Caucasus.

"When our ancestors," says the Kabardian
bards, " inhabited the shores of the sea of Azow,
the isles of Taman, and the Tanais, they had frequent wars with the Emazuhnites, (Amazonian
women,) who lived contiguous to the mountain region we now occupy.   No men were permitted to
reside among them ; but every woman, of whatever
nation, desirous of assisting them in their predatory enterprises, and of conforming to their laws
and customs, was most cordially welcomed.   After
a series of successes and defeats on both sides, it

happened, when the two armies were opposite
each other, and on the point of coming to a general engagement, Valdusa, a famous heroine
and a prophetess, much celebrated among her
sister warriors, suddenly rushed forward on her
prancing charger, and requested an interview with
Thulme, the commander of the Circassians, who,
it appears, was also endued with the prophetic
spirit.

" A tent having been pitched in the central
space between the two armies, the generals, mas-
culine and feminine, commenced their conference.
That they discussed other topics than such as related to war may be inferred from the result, for
after prolonging the conference to several hours,
they had talked themselves into such an unanimity of opinion, that, upon coming forth, they
declared to their respective armies that the gods
had commanded a cessation of hostilities, and as
a preliminary of peace, they themselves had
agreed to marry, at the same time recommending
their armies to follow so pacific an example. The
belligerents, wisely considering this to be a very
agreeable method of terminating hostilities,
adopted it without hesitation ; and the Circassians, finding that the country of their warlike

brides was strongly defended by nature, established themselves in it, which they have ever since continued to inhabit."

This tradition, singularly enough, corresponds with the relation of Herodotus concerning the Amazons : " When the Greeks," says that historian, " fought against the Amazons, whom they termed Androchtones, (slayers of men,) and defeated them on the banks of the Thermodon, they carried off three ships loaded with their fair prisoners. During the voyage the refractory fair ones rebelled against their gaolers, and, utterly in defiance of the dictates of gentleness or humanity, massacred the whole. It is true, the lady warriors gained their liberty, but, being entirely ignorant of navigation, the ships were left to the mercy of the winds and waves, which finally drove them into the Maeotian sea, (sea of Azow,) and they landed at Cremnes, in the country of the Scythians."

The next act of these merciless damsels was to seize all the horses they could find, plunder the country, and slay such of the inhabitants as opposed them. The Scythians, upon discovering the sex and beauty of their feminine invaders, summoned a council, when was it resolved, by the elders of the land, to try another method of subduing them; this was, to send a body of their finest young men to encamp in their immediate neighbourhood, with strict orders to treat them with uniform kindness, and, if possible, so far to win their confidence as to obtain them in marriage.

From whatever cause, the Scythians contrived to render themselves more amiable in the eyes of their fair foes than the Greeks, the plan completely succeeded, for the camps daily approached nearer to each other, and the treaty of peace was signed at the altar of Hymen; each Scythian won for himself an Amazonian bride, and thus founded the powerful nation of the Sauromatians (Sarmatians.)

The whole of the Greek writers of that epoch confirm this statement, particularly Skymnos of Chio, who says, "In Scythia, to the north of the Caucasus, have dwelt, from time immemorial, the nation of the Maeotians, who have given their name to the sea in their vicinity, Palus Maeotis; adjoining and their territory beyond the Tanais (Don), in Asia, lies the country of the Sauromatians, or Gynaiko Kralumenoi (a people ruled by women)."

We have also the authority of Hyporcrates, who says, that there is a tribe of Scythians inhabiting the coast of the Palus Maeotis, whose customs and manners differ entirely from those of their neighbours : the women are accomplished, not only as equestrians, but as archers,—march to battle against their enemies, their laws compelling them to remain unmarried till they were so fortunate as to kill one of their foes in battle.

Is there not, therefore, strong reason for conjecturing, from the history of the ancients and the traditions of the Kabardians, and from the circumstance that the two Kabardahs and the adjoining mountains were the original country of the Amazons,—that the Attéghéi tribes at present inhabiting the Western Caucasus are the original stock of Sarmatians, the descendants of the Scythian Maeotian youths and their warlike brides, the Amazons, who, it appears, were neither Greek nor Maeotian, but in all probability of Median extraction, for Herodotus expressly says, that the Maeotians spoke a corrupt dialect of the Scythian, which their Amazonian wives never could learn correctly, and the Greek writers, when describing the defeat of the Amazons on the banks of the Thermodon, inform us that they were the widows and daughters of a band of freebooters, whose male protectors having been slain in battle, they flew to arms. The same authors also relate that they belonged to a foreign colony from a distant land, that had settled on the plains of Themiskéré, on the coast of Capadocia, in Asia Minor.

CHAPTER IV.

Advantages of a commercial alliance between Great Britain
and Circassia—Productions of that country—Its natural
harbours—Aggressions of Russia—Gross injustice of that
power towards the Caucasians—The importance of the
Caucasus to Russia—Rivalry between England and Russia
—Moral influence of England—Vacillating policy of the
English Government.

HAVING disposed of the question relative to the
origin of the Circassians, we shall next proceed to
the consideration of the commercial and political
advantages which might be derived from establishing a friendly intercourse between that people
and England,—an intercourse which they, on their
part, have appeared most anxious to cultivate,
even to the extent of placing their country under
the protection of Great Britain ; and how desirable
is it at the present moment, when nearly the whole
of Europe have commenced manufacturing their

own wares, that we should connect ourselves with those regions or states whose wants may give employment to, and whose productions may supply the demands of, a manufacturing people.

Circassia fulfils both these characters: the people manufacture nothing save a few articles of the first necessity, and ornaments, which would in no way interfere with ours; at the same time the country is fertile to exuberance, and being nearly in a state of nature with regard to its mineral productions, &c., the resources it offers to speculative and well-directed enterprise are incalculable.   It ought also to be borne in mind, that the long line of the Circassian coast is furnished with numerous natural harbours, most of which are protected from violent winds, and afford good anchorage.

If the cruel war which now desolates her valleys were terminated, we might obtain, in exchange for our own commodities, abundance of the finest wool, tallow, hides, furs, &c.,—articles for which we are obliged to pay Russia and other countries with specie.   Besides these, the country abounds with every description of timber, now left to decay for the want of an outlet; the oak, valona, and box, alone, before Russia appropriated the

navigation of the Euxine to herself, were sources
of immense profit to the Turks, the surplus of
which they were accustomed to dispose of to the
foreign traders at Constantinople.

Circassia also produces grain of excellent quality, and the tobacco is much esteemed for its
fragrance; for these the Turks also bartered salt,
gunpowder, fire-arms, cloths, and calicoes. The
whole of this lucrative trade might be secured
to England, were the tyrannical blockade removed from her coasts, which could be easily
effected through prompt energetic measures on
the part of our government, without even the
necessity of war, Circassia being strong enough
to defend herself, if once decisively countenanced
by the sympathy and moral support of England.
The first step should be, to acknowledge the
independence of Circassia,—in fact, nothing more
than an act of strict justice, due from one independent nation to another,—and then, by the
weight and influence of our representations with
the European powers, terminate a barbarous, unjust war, disgraceful to the civilized age in which
we live—a war, as barbarous, and far more unjust,
than that of the Turks, which depopulated the
fair fields of unhappy Greece, with this difference,

that we must admit—notwithstanding the sympathy which we naturally felt, and must ever feel, for the Greeks—that they were rebels in arms against their lawful sovereign, while the Circassians, on the contrary, are an independent people, bravely fighting for life and liberty against a power who, in defiance of all law, human and divine, seeks to rob them of what the brave and the free hold dearer than life itself—home and country. Yet Russia is a power who arrogates to herself a character for humanity, and a consideration for the rights of nations : did she not, during the contest between Greece and Turkey, assume (to conceal her own selfish purposes) the mask of Christian philanthropy, and preach her hypocritical crusade through the instrumentality of her clever agents, till she gained over, not only the whole of the press, but the great powers of Europe, to her views. The result is a matter of history ; Greece was declared independent, and the last remnant of Turkish power annihilated in the bay of Navarino.

Let it not, however, be understood, that in making these observations I sympathize with the Turks, or their barbarous butcheries in Greece ; I have merely mentioned the subject by way of illustration, to elucidate Russian intrigue and the folly of her infatuated dupes ; for the same power who, under the disguise of Christian philanthropy, enlisted Europe in her cause, now equals, if not exceeds, the infidel Turks in the work of spoliation and massacre in the Caucasian provinces. Yet, with the exception of the press of England and France, not a single voice has been raised in behalf of that country—not a single power (for the sake of humanity) has remonstrated with Russia.

It would appear, indeed, as if the whole of Europe at the present moment were governed by statesmen either supine, negligent, or incompetent; or as if they were afraid, by raising the voice of censure, they should draw down upon themselves a frown from the despot of the north. France, Austria, and England, cannot view with any degree of complacency the menacing character of the Russian armaments in the Baltic and the Black Sea, nor the near accomplishment of her designs on Circassia—a possession which would at once insure to her the real sovereignty of Turkey and Persia, and then, colossus-like, with one foot in Europe, and the other in Asia, should dictate laws to their commerce, and rule in their councils.

A very different line of conduct was pursued

towards the Ottoman Porte, already sunk low in feebleness and decay, as if that fact alone should invite their hostility, during her contest with her revolted subjects in Greece. Then Europe echoed from one end to the other with her supposed and real barbarities; but Turkey had no clever ambassadors to cajole and deceive; no accomplished princesses to send intriguing from court to court; no brilliant crosses and jewelled orders to bestow on those who could advance her interest, and aid her measures; no splendid court with which to dazzle and flatter;—in short, from her faith, manners, and customs, she was an alien among the nations; a prize to be divided among those whose cupidity might blind them to their future interest, in assisting in her spoliation. But, as I before observed, it is not so with Russia. That pretended supporter of thrones and social order may plunder, slay, imprison and confiscate, beard and insult, with impunity. Even in our own country, do we not see, with regret and astonishment, the representative of the freest nation in the world, the recognised chief of the liberal party, publicly lauding the acts and policy of a sovereign who, however amiable he might be in private life, in

his character of chief of the Russian empire is
placed in a situation which compels him, by the
march of events, and the voice of his people, to
seek our overthrow. England, that stumbling-
block to her schemes of aggrandizement and
oppression, is hated by Russia; for she knows
that England abhors despotism, and that her
generous sons, alone among the nations, fear-
lessly promulgate her crimes to the world; with
them, jewelled orders and courtly blandishments
are but as the baubles of women and empty
compliments.

But I regret to say that we cannot here end
our censures of the un-English—un-statesman-
like policy that has recently guided some of
our rulers. The same courtly flattery that won
our representative at St. Petersburg seems to
have travelled to our own land, and so completely
to have fascinated her Majesty's advisers that
we see with pain a minister whose denunci-
ations against Russian aggression were a hundred times boldly hurled in the presence of the
British senate—though he sees his country degraded and insulted, her merchantmen captured
on the high seas, and her enterprising citizens,
while exercising their rights as traders, pinioned

as felons and consigned to dungeons—openly
defending that aggression in parliament, declaring his countrymen contrabandists, and de-
nouncing as rebels the unfortunate inhabitants
of the country it was his duty to countenance
and, if necessary, to protect.

Thus he has given the whole weight, influence,
and support of Great Britain to Russia; has
encouraged her to seize and confiscate our vessels under any pretence, however unfounded;
and openly granted her a carte blanche to pursue her projects of aggrandizement in the East
and elsewhere.

Must we not pronounce this declaration to be
impolitic and uncalled for? a declaration that
will travel from sea to sea, from land to land,
from Europe to Asia, and produce more advantageous results to the ambitious projects of the
autocrat of Russia than the most brilliant victory
his arms could achieve. It will sound as the
death-knell in the ears of the sons of hapless
Poland, astound and bewilder the too-confiding
Turk, and blast the hopes of the Circassians.

This subserviency to Russian interests is a
new feature in the policy of our government
—a coalition with despotism as unnatural as it

is unwise, which I will endeavour hereafter to prove ; and however much it may contribute to maintain her Majesty's ministers in office, prognosticates evil rather than good to the country, and must necessarily be viewed by the people of England with distrust.

We have the evidence of experience to prove that Russia never submitted to humiliation, except for the prospect of some ulterior advantage ; and her union with the actual government of England, whose ministers have repeatedly assailed her with every abusive epithet that language could supply, shews that the object she has now in view is one of paramount importance. It is therefore evident that, unless speedy and decisive measures are adopted to counteract the ascendancy of Russian influence in our cabinet, we shall see ourselves again, for the hundredth time, rendered instrumental in advancing the interests of our most subtle enemy.

I would ask my readers, what unanimity of opinion, what reciprocity of friendship, can possibly exist between two powers so diametrically opposed to each other in policy, government, and institutions, as England and Russia ? We see their interests, political and commercial,

jarring in every part of the world; each jealous
of the influence, and suspicious of the designs,
of the other; both powerful empires; if the one
preponderates in numerical force, wealth and
intelligence establish and uphold the ascendancy
of the other. Constitutional England, guided
and governed by institutions based upon rational
liberty, applies herself to the reason of man,
and seeks, by argument and a public exposition
of her acts, to win his assent to the measures
she proposes; her aim is to lead on the human
mind till it adopts, through conviction, the
opinions she labours to instil; and thus she
gains her point without having occasion to resort
to coercive measures.

On the other hand, Russia, like every other
despotic power having a ruler without responsibility, an aristocracy without control, and a
democracy without a voice in the disposal of
their lives and properties, exercises, owing to
her system of governing, no moral influence
upon the minds of the enlightened inhabitants of
Europe, nor upon those of the intellectual and
the educated among her own subjects, who, finding themselves humiliated and debased, will ever
seek to subvert a government unprovided with

any other aid to carry its measures into effect than brute force.

In short, wherever the human intellect is in advance, it will naturally ally itself with freedom; and it is only by keeping it stationary (a somewhat difficult undertaking) that despotism can hope to reign in tranquillity; the wisest plans, however, will fail to accomplish this; and for the simple reason, that the character of mutation is stamped upon all that is human, moral as well as physical. Even if there were no intellectual force to propel man forward in his career of improvement, steam navigation and commerce will effect this in due time; the most dangerous enemies that despotism has to fear.

It is scarcely necessary to add that powers governed in every act by such opposing principles as England and Russia must be hostile to each other. England cannot retrograde; despotism cannot live, much less flourish, in a land that has been so long familiar with the blessings of freedom, where every institution, public and private, is wedded to rational liberty, and whose sons taught the world that a people could be free without plunging into anarchy or producing a revolutionary chaos.

It is owing to the liberal institutions of England, and the well-ordered system she has organized—which, although foreign to everything in the shape of tyranny or arbitrary measures, maintains her laws, and advances the prosperity and civilization of her people,—that the surrounding nations have regarded her with admiration, not unmixed with jealousy, and have sought, and ever will seek, as they advance in civilization and intelligence, to emancipate themselves from slavery, and establish a similar form of government, which tends so much to elevate man to that state of independence for which nature had destined him as a rational being.

It must therefore be obvious that England, from the nature of the principles by which she is actuated, becomes, independently of any volition of her own, the natural chief of constitutional liberty throughout the world, the great bulwark against despotism—a position which, if her rulers were sagacious enough to avail themselves of, would undoubtedly impart to her an influence in the affairs of Europe more commanding, more extensive, than any other nation has ever enjoyed, for it is the dominion of *truth* and *mind*.

The command, I had almost said the absolute command, she exercises, or ought to exercise, over the destinies of the nations, must be apparent, when we remember that the inhabitants of Europe are now divided into two great sections, constitutionalists and absolutists. This being admitted, we may, without fear of contradiction, infer that the next general war (religious considerations being now no longer of paramount importance) will have its origin in the principles of liberty and despotism. It is the fear of this war of principle that haunts the despotic powers,— that has maintained peace during the various great changes that have recently taken place —the revolutions in France, Belgium, Spain, and elsewhere,—all of which have been, in a greater or less degree, destructive of the interests of despotic rule. It is by means of this fear that Great Britain, if her councils were directed by a man of genius, would exercise her influence, and infuse terror into the cabinets of her rivals, for they too well know that a rupture with her would accelerate, if not produce, the dreaded revolutionary burst of *freedom or death!*

This was the view taken by the immortal Canning of the state of Europe, when he made

his famous declaration in reference to the South
American States—a declaration which shook the
throne of every despotic monarch in Europe;
and how easy would it have been for that great
statesman, if he had deemed it expedient to
ensure the success of his measures, to fan into a
flame the embers of constitutional liberty. During his energetic administration, England was
looked up to with respect and reverence by the
surrounding nations, not so much for her great
military fame as the conqueror of Napoleon,
not more for her wealth and resources, than for
the principles she professes. She was feared by
despotism, and regarded by those persecuted for
the cause of liberty as the palladium of their hopes,
their refuge in the time of need, whose countenance kept alive hope, and awed their oppressors;
but, alas! that influence exists no more; it lies
buried in the grave of Poland! The sceptre of
power which our ever-to-be-lamented statesman
so successfully wielded, and which had so long
influenced Europe and Asia, we see in our day
broken in pieces, and the respect with which
we were then regarded as a nation converted
into undisguised contempt.

If a weak, timid, vacillating policy has rendered Great Britain despised in Europe, it has reduced her still lower in Asia; for, from the moment the Russian hosts marched to the aid of Turkey's helpless Sultan, who vainly implored our assistance, to which we may add our never-to-be-forgotten disgrace in the Euxine, the charm which had so long given efficacy to our councils, and might to our influence, in the East, lost its potency and effect. This feeling, it is but too probable, will spread from city to city, from land to land, till at length it will reach the indolent inhabitants of our vast territories in Asia, encourage them to rebel, and for ever sever the slender thread that binds them to our empire.

CHAPTER V.

Ancient settlements of the Genoese in the Western Caucasus
—Great sources of wealth to that people—Hostility of
Russia towards Great Britain—Advantages to England
of preserving the Caucasian isthmus independent—
Ambitious views of the Russian government—Predator
disposition of the Russian people—Their desire to invade
India.

But to return to Circassia. The interruption of
the commerce which our enterprising merchants
had so happily commenced with that country
will, I fear, prove an irreparable injury to our
trading interests. The Genoese, who were perfectly aware of the natural advantages possessed
by the countries on the Black Sea, at an early
epoch, formed commercial establishments on its
coasts, which subsequently proved mines of wealth
to that republic of traders, and contributed to
exalt it, through the commercial spirit of its
citizens, from an insignificant commonwealth to

one of the most influential states that existed
during the middle ages, whose fleets and armies
were the dread of the surrounding nations ; and
does not England herself owe the whole of her
wealth and greatness to the same source ? yet, in
the nineteenth century, can it be believed that,
with all our sagacity and wisdom, with the example of our forefathers to instruct us, an opportunity is wilfully lost of extending our commerce,
enriching our people, and increasing our influence.

Our government, nay, every well-educated man
in the empire at all conversant with the existing
relations between the Russian government and
the Caucasus, must be aware that Circassia is an
independent country : by simply recognising her
as such we should at once further our interests,
rescue a brave people from the sword of their
destroyer, win their eternal gratitude, and the
applause of admiring Europe.

If such a declaration were made by a power
possessed of the weight and influence of Great
Britain, Russia durst not fire another gun on
their shores, nor continue to blockade their coasts;
for, independent of any other consideration, the
reproaches and maledictions of indignant Europe

would operate so powerfully as a check upon
her ambitious designs against her unequal adver-
sary, as effectually to put a stop to further hostilities. That power, which is, as it were, emerging
from barbarism, being sensitively apprehensive of
outraging public opinion, would, at least, substitute intrigue and bribery for the sword,—Circassia
being too valuable a prize to be wholly relinquished.

Some of my contemporaries, when reviewing
my late work, seemed to infer from its tenour that
I was an advocate for war; they are wholly mistaken, for I am fully assured, that even if England
were to send a fleet to-morrow into the Euxine,
it would not be followed by any more hostile
demonstration on the part of Russia than an
attempt to bully by a bombardment of protocols.
That government, as I have already observed,
dare not go to war at the present moment with
any of the first-rate powers of Europe. She
" bides her time." This position of affairs, however, cannot last for ever, and when a collision
does take place, a sanguinary and protracted
struggle will follow, terminating in the utter
humiliation of one power or the other; and fate
appears to have placed England and Russia in a

position which, at no distant period, must lead to hostilities.

Assuming, therefore, from the elements of discord existing between us, that a commotion must inevitably ensue, how necessary is it that we should be prepared with some effectual means of subduing the approaching evil? Judging from the present aspect of affairs, it is highly probable that the first hostile attempt will be made upon our Asiatic possessions, as the most vulnerable, and as affording no inconsiderable share of valuable plunder to her half-disciplined, needy, marauding, hordes of soldiers.

In anticipation of this evil, we should lose no time in strengthening our resources in the East; in forming alliances with the various nations and wandering tribes through whose dominions her armies must necessarily pass. Commercial treaties, tending to establish a good understanding, should be entered into with Turkey and Persia. However weak they may be in their present state, however servilely they may now crouch to their powerful neighbour, they nevertheless cherish towards their ancient enemy a hatred deep-rooted and implacable.

Let it also be remembered, that a Mahometan,

in compliance with the tenets of his faith, never forgives an injury; with him blood can never be atoned for but by blood, and if circumstances prevent him during life from obtaining satisfaction, he bequeaths his insatiable desire for revenge as a legacy to his descendants. Another tenet of the Mahometan is, that he never considers himself deprived of the right and title to any possessions which have been wrung from him either by conquest or treaty; consequently, he is always ready to seize any favourable moment for the recovery of his losses.

The immense advantages we derived from our alliances with Spain and Portugal during the late war, are well known, and ought to be our guide in the present aspect of affairs in the East. Since that great contest for European independence, political interests have entirely changed; for although the empire of the mighty chief who then directed the destinies of Europe exists no more, the sceptre of ambition that so long convulsed the world was not destroyed—it has passed into the hands of another power, and that power is Russia. We may therefore confidently anticipate, that the arena of the next general war will be principally confined to those countries in the neighbourhood of the Black Sea —there will be fought the great battle which is to decide the fate of nations.

Above all, and at every hazard, Circassia should be preserved independent. That strong hold, with its inaccessible defiles and manly inhabitants, offers a *pied de terre* of more value to England than Turkey herself, with her indolent effendis and servile rajahs. There we might, at any time, and for a trifling expense, owing to the warlike disposition of the people, their simple habits, and abstemious mode of living, organize and equip two hundred thousand of the bravest troops in the universe, capable of carrying fire and sword, should such an extreme measure be deemed necessary, on to the very gates of Moscow.

Already, unassisted and deficient in all the *materiel* of war, we see the confederated tribes of the Caucasus victorious in almost every engagement with the well-disciplined troops of their invader ; and such has been their devotedness and gigantic efforts in the cause of liberty and fatherland, that the contest, which has been hitherto confined to the Western Caucasus, now rages on the shores of the Caspian Sea. Entire tribes, and the inhabitants of whole provinces, which, till very recently, acknowledged the supremacy of Russia, have flown to arms; even the forts on the great military road, the Wladi Kaukas, leading to Georgia, are in a state of siege. In addition to these, thousands of Polish and Russian deserters have joined, and continue to join, the standard of the patriots, a circumstance which has, in no inconsiderable degree, contributed to render ineffectual the utmost efforts of the Russian generals to penetrate, much less subdue, a single province.

If such has been the success of the mountaineers, notwithstanding all the disadvantages under which they labour, what might not their success be were they countenanced even by the moral support, not to mention the actual assistance, of England. The mere presence of a British fleet in the Euxine would be the signal for Turk, Persian, and those Krim Tartars that now acknowledge Russian authority, simultaneously to arm; and the result would probably be, the retreat of Russia to her own snowy steppes, and the establishment of European peace on a foundation at once solid and durable; for too certain it is, unless that power receives a check in her ambitious career, we cannot calculate, with any degree of probability, that the gates of Janus will long remain closed, that the present Augustan age will long continue to shed its blessings over civilized Europe.

To arrest the encroachments of Russia, and frustrate her designs of conquest in the East, is at once our interest and duty; it is our interest, because, if left to pursue her course without interruption, she will, independent of any other mischief which may accrue, forestall our commerce in the market of every country over which she may acquire influence; aye, and take her measures so adroitly that we shall find, when it is too late, we are entirely excluded; for the councils of Russia are directed with no inconsiderable portion of the wisdom of the serpent, well knowing that commerce has been the great source of our wealth, the mainspring of our national prosperity.

It is our duty, inasmuch as it is an obligation (apart from any commercial interest) imposed upon us, from our rank and influence among the nations, to procure, for the sake of humanity, a cessation of hostilities in Circassia, and a removal of the atrocious blockade.

We should also endeavour to enlighten the

benighted inhabitants of that portion of the globe,
by imparting to them our laws and institutions;
for however imperfect these may be when compared with the ideal standard of what they might
be rendered, they are yet founded in wisdom,
tested by experience, and have confessedly a direct tendency to propel man onward in the path
of civilization.

This civilization and enlightenment will be best
insured by establishing with them commercial relations, which would answer the twofold purpose
of enriching them, and, as they advance in industry and wealth, of rendering the barrier still more
formidable against the inroads of that only European power which seeks, through its wanton
aggression and insatiable ambition, to disturb the
harmony of nations.

It is also our duty, and one of the first importance, to maintain our East India possessions, and
secure and protect them from aggression; for, to
say nothing of the immense mass of British property, public and private, vested there, we are
imperatively bound, by every motive of justice
and humanity towards the hundred millions of
subjects who look up to us for protection, to watch
over their safety, and shield them from all the

horrors attendant on foreign invasion.   This
would be accomplished, with every certainty
of success, by attaching Circassia to our interests, while we stand upon our present vantage
ground.

We have already shewn that a possession so
valuable in the present state of affairs may be acquired without even the loss of a single British
subject, in consequence of the sympathy manifested by the inhabitants of the Western Caucasus
for England, and the desire they have evinced to
place themselves under her fostering care.   But
we must not hesitate ; if the present opportunity
be lost, it will pass away never to return.   However resolute and successful that noble people may
have hitherto been in defending their country
against tyrannical and unjust invasion,—and however much the unanimity of purpose resulting
from the confederation of its various tribes promises success in their desperate struggle,—still
the consciousness of utter abandonment by England, to whom all eyes have been directed, may
paralyze their efforts, may ultimately cause their
irretrievable fall.   And were they not virtually
abandoned when our minister made his uncalled
for declaration in parliament in favour of his new

ally?—a declaration which may, ere this, have reached the Caucasus, and produced the extinction of hope—that spell which, when once lost, either by nations or individuals, gives place to the torpid numbness of despair.

Without hope, all strength, moral as well as physical, avails nothing; and should Circassia, at a later period, be added to the already overgrown possessions of our too subtle enemy, I do not hesitate to assert that achievement has been consummated by her Majesty's ministers,—an achievement which Russia never could effect by force of arms; and should the results I have predicted be too faithfully realized, how fearful may be the consequences to posterity of their mistaken views!

We know that the object the government have in view is the preservation of peace, to conciliate the anti-war party, and the repugnance entertained by a large majority to interpose in the affairs of foreign nations. How vain are their hopes! how futile their endeavours! They ought to take example from the story of the Man and the Ass in the fable, for, by their timid measures, and endeavours to maintain peace, they only increase the evil by deferring it to a future day,—for at an earlier or a later period war is inevitable; I say,

at an earlier or a later period we shall be called
upon to defend our eastern empire,—an empire
that has been in every age the magnet of attraction to the half-military half-savage tribes that
have desolated the earth in their marauding expeditions in search of plunder, and is now coveted
with the keenest desire by the semi-barbarous
hordes of Russia; a desire which that power
takes good care to propagate among her needy
subjects,—India sounding as welcome to the ears
of a Cossack as the merry peal announcing his
marriage does to him who is on the point of being
united to the object of his fondest wishes. I have
often seen these fellows,—who, to say the truth,
are accused of being somewhat given to rapine in
their military expeditions,—at the mere mention
of a prospect of marching to the land of pearls and
diamonds, caper like so many half-crazy dervishes.

The Emperor of Russia, a really amiable man
in private life, with every disposition to preserve
peace, cannot pause in his march of aggression;
the slave of a million of bayonets and an ambitious aristocracy, his own life and the safety of
his empire are involved in the question of war or
peace. Whether his career may prove ruinous
or glorious, futurity will reveal; he cannot, how-

ever, remain inactive; for such have been the repeated victories obtained by the Russian troops during his reign over their degenerate neighbours, the inhabitants of Turkey and Persia, and the plunder they obtained in these countries has so excited their cupidity, that they now naturally desire a war with any power by which they are likely to reap a rich harvest.

I repeat, the Emperor of Russia must advance; any symptom of wavering, any check to the progress of the mighty engine of which he is the compulsory director, would burst forth in plots, conspiracies, assassinations, &c.; in short, in all the horrors a discontented soldiery are capable of perpetrating. Conscious of this, and knowing that the existence of himself and empire depends upon the influence of the sword, he indulges the hope, on the subjugation of the Caucasus, that path to conquest and supreme dominion, of being enabled to give full employment to his marauding myrmidons.

His first step, of course, would be to take possession of Constantinople and the Levant; then, with Herat on one side, and the Oxus on the other, we might as well preach silence to the

winds of heaven as to attempt to arrest his progress to India.

Having already endeavoured, without success,
to impress the facts and opinions here stated upon
more than one of her Majesty's advisers, who appear to be either completely fettered by their union
with a certain "no war" party, or entangled in
the meshes of Muscovite intrigue, I would address
myself to my compatriots in general. I would
appeal to their feelings, being certain that, when
the Circassian question is thoroughly understood,
there will be a reaction. Can there be a doubt
that a nation which has ever been the protector
of the weak and oppressed, ever foremost in the
cause of freedom and humanity, will respond to
the call of a noble, a persecuted people? It is
contrary to the generous spirit of Britons to remain cold spectators of a contest so unequal,
so atrocious, and one in which their own interests are involved. I would also return my sin-
cerest thanks to the press, particularly that portion in the Conservative interest, for seconding
with such manly zeal and ability my feeble efforts
in endeavouring to arouse public sympathy in
favour of Circassia, and spreading so widely the

knowledge of their real situation. Continue your
generous efforts (they will raise to your party a
host of friends who are now wavering, for they
breathe intelligence and sentiments of the purest
patriotism,) until not only England, but the whole
of chivalrous Europe, is roused in behalf of justice
and humanity.

I cannot, however, conclude these observations
without quoting the words of a writer on the
Circassian question in one of the most intelligent
periodicals of the day,* which, for truly English
sentiment, just views, and generous feeling, cannot be exceeded; and those persons who still
doubt the necessity of our government pursuing
rigorous measures in the east, and the expediency
of preserving Circassia independent, I would
counsel to peruse and re-peruse this article, instead of exclaiming, with a sneer of ignorance,
What are the savages of the Caucasus to us?
What advantages, political or commercial, can
be derived from an intercourse with a nation of
freebooting robbers?—sentiments so un-English

* The article on Circassia, in the November and December
numbers of Blackwood's Magazine, 1837.

must assuredly have been learned from the Russian catechism.

"If, on the other hand," says our clever advocate for the independence of the Caucasian Isthmus, "Russia succeed in subjugating Circassia, whether by extirmination or by exhausting the spirit and resources of its warlike clans, thus abandoned to an interminable and hopeless struggle, it must be obvious that no possible event could contribute so greatly to the success of her gigantic projects: secure from the dangers attendant on leaving an active enemy in her rear, and of having the communications of her trans-Caucasian army with southern Russia cut off,—with every route by sea or land wide open to facilitate her military movements or transport of stores, and with the additional advantage of having a large body of troops placed at her disposal by the termination of a bloody and disastrous war,—she could then at pleasure move forward her forces, and attack Persia on a scale which the present fetters on her power, and the want of resources in her trans-Caucasian provinces, would prevent her now from doing."

The occupation of Turkish-Armenia, and the

seizure of Trebizond, with the whole intervening
coast of the Black Sea, might be made simultaneous with an attack on the line of the Arras,
and Turkey fettered while Persia was irretriev-
ably overwhelmed.

The vision of European statesmen in general
seems never to penetrate into Asia. A political
mist hovers over the eastern shore of the Bosphorus, which blinds them to all that may pass
beyond it. It is from the side of Europe alone that
they contemplate danger to Turkey—to Constantinople—from Russia. Far otherwise is it with
those of Russia; full well do they know the se-
crets of the Asiatic shore, and the importance of
a footing there; for though they feel that another
systematic attack upon the European provinces
of Turkey, or a coup-de-main upon the Turkish
capital, would be vain while the eyes of Europe
are upon her, they know that, deprived of the
resources of Anatolia, Constantinople must soon
fall, while approaches from that quarter would
create neither alarm nor opposition from the other
powers; and the agents of Russia themselves
have been heard to declare that her next operations against Turkey *should be through Asia
Minor*. But *while Circassia remains unsubdued in*

her rear, such approaches on the part of Russia
are impossible.*

" If in what has been said we have made ourselves at all understood, it must appear that the
Caucasian Isthmus, and Circassia in particular, is
the key to all the projected enterprises of Russia
in the East, and that to obtain it is for her a
stern political necessity. But while every motive
of interest, and ambition, and jealous rivalry,
impels the cabinet of St. Petersburg to spare no
cost for its acquirement, does it not follow that
those whom her projects, if successful, would
vitally injure, are equally interested in resisting,
as far as in them lies, this fatal consummation,
and in preserving the Circassian independence?
To Great Britain, in particular, the success of the

---

* There are only two roads across the Caucasus, the
Wladi Kaukas and that by Derbend on the Caspian Sea, by
which military stores and supplies for an army can be transported; and these are liable to be interrupted by the unceasing hostilities of the mountaineers, who still hold possession of the whole of the passes. Russia is equally unfortunate by way of the Black Sea; she may, it is true, land
supplies on the beach in Mingrelia, but further she cannot
advance without a powerful armed escort, so long as the
fierce tribes of Abasia continue to inhabit the mountains that
domineer over the country.

Circassian cause must be held of first-rate importance, for Circassia is, in truth, the point of most
immediate importance to the security of her
Indian dominions, and to the maintenance of that
high position she has held and ought to support
in Central Asia."

CHAPTER VI.

Conflicting opinions respecting Russian policy and the invasion of India—The duty of England to protect that empire—Colonies proved to be a source of wealth to the
mother country—Preliminary steps of Russia towards
the invasion of India—Plan of invasion contemplated by
the Emperor Paul—How to prevent the invasion of
India.

I AM aware that my opinions respecting the
ambitious views of Russia, the extension of her
dominions in Asia, and the probability of an
attack, at some future period, upon our Indian
possessions, will be deemed by some chimerical,
by others, demonstrative of the presence of a
violent infliction of Russo-phobia,—and this by
men whose admitted abilities and recognised intelligence gives weight and authority to their
opinions.

On these points I must beg leave to differ from
my opponents, and future events will, I fear, too

fatally prove my predictions to be realized, unless strong measures are immediately adopted to arrest the evil.

In the present day, few, unfortunately, even of our most intelligent writers, are conversant with the real state of Central Asia; while others, grounding their conclusions upon the extensive line of Russian frontier, her thinly scattered population, their poverty and clashing interests, upon the inadequacy of the resources of the empire to its wants, and the selfish peculation of the civil and military employées, tell us that she is already hastening to her fall.

These arguments, I regret to say, however well-intentioned they may be, have a direct tendency to deceive the people of England as to the real character of Russian policy, and to prevent the exercise of due caution by preparing to meet any sudden collision that might take place between us and that power; not, however, that I am one of those who anticipate a descent upon our own sea-girt isle. But we should not allow ourselves to be deluded by such arguments and misrepresentations; it is incumbent upon us to provide for every contingency, however remote; a danger for which adequate provision is made beforehand, ceases to become one; and the trifling expense we should at present incur by strengthening our navy, would produce the most important results.

Instead of parading in the Mediterranean and the Tagus, let a competent marine force dash into the Euxine, and decide the question at once; break the bands that bind Turkey and Persia to their hereditary foe, and tell the world from henceforth that the Euxine shall be a highway for the nations. This, indeed, would be the determination of a statesman gifted with the intellectual grasp of a Pitt or a Canning; then would India be preserved, the mist that hovers round the Caucasus and Central Asia removed, and a new channel opened for our commerce, which would insure to our descendants incalculable wealth.

Again, I have been assured by some of my contemporaries, that even were Russia in possession of the whole coast of the Black Sea, of Constantinople, Persia, and the Caucasus, no danger could exist of her invading India. What, we are told, are there no impassable deserts, no valiant independent tribes, no broad rivers and snowy Alps, no inhospitable regions, to be passed by an invading army? How are they to obtain provisions ; how transport the stores necessary for an army to attempt a conquest of such magnitude ?

Let the existence of all these obstacles be admitted ; let them prove the enterprise to be one of difficulty ; it does not follow that it is impossible. Every great conqueror recorded in the annals of Asiatic warfare succeeded in carrying his arms into Hindostan, from Alexander, the Macedonian, to Genghis-Khan, the Mongul Tartar, down to the Persian adventurer, Nadir Shah, who, with his limited resources, fought his way to the capital, Delhi, which he sacked, and returned with a booty valued at the immense sum of more than eighty-seven millions and a half sterling.*

We cannot feel surprised at the conflicting opinions entertained upon this subject when we remember the importance of the question involved. It is natural that the possibility of the invasion of India, whether by Russia or any other power, should be a matter of deep interest to the English nation ; particularly to those persons who have long resided in India, or who feel

* See Mr. Baillie Frazer's interesting work, the ' Persian Adventurer.'

anxious for the welfare of others bound up with
the prosperity of that empire.

On the other hand, we have a party at home,
of late years on the increase, some of whose
tenets I cannot but consider dangerously erroneous, who maintain that the country would be
more prosperous without India, or, indeed, any
other of our colonies; regarding them as a
cause of loss, and not a source of gain, to the
mother country. Now our opinion, and it is
hoped and presumed that of the great majority
of the nation, is diametrically opposed to this.
We deem India and our other colonies to be the
real sources of our wealth,—to protect them from
invasion, a duty from which we cannot shrink.

The consideration, that India, and indeed the
whole of our colonies, as they increase in power,
wealth, and population, will become, as a matter
of course, successively independent, ought not
to deter us from extending towards them our
fostering care; from cherishing them as our offspring, who, when arrived at maturity and competent to provide for themselves, may be left to
their own resources. But will not the same
reciprocal affection still exist; the same community of interests, the consequence of a long

commercial intercourse, of their speaking the same language, and being governed by the same laws and institutions; and will it not be impossible to separate this community of interests, so closely linked, so mutually advantageous?

In proof of this, we have only to refer to the United States of America: although we did not act towards that child of our creation with the moderation and forbearance which wisdom, and indeed duty, required,—although we provoked a whole people to assert their independence by arms, and although this war was succeeded by all the heart-burnings and revengeful feelings which a sense of injury and tyrannical measures could create, still they never did, never can, forget the land, the home, of their ancestors; and we now carry on a commerce with them more profitable and extensive than with any other country of a similar population. We should, therefore, endeavour to sow the seeds of concord and kindness, eradicate whatever irritated feelings may still remain—a duty incumbent on all who desire the prosperity and the friendship of a people who, from their growing power and influence, may hereafter be in a situation to render us the most important benefits.

The final results will, in all probability, be similar, as regards those colonies which we still retain. It is, however, to be hoped, with the example of the errors of our fathers to instruct us, that we shall rule with mildness, and, instead of having recourse to coercive measures, retain them in allegiance by the firm, but gentle, exercise of parental authority, which cannot fail of attaching them to a country to which they owe everything. Besides, we shall have the gratification of being powerfully instrumental in civilizing the world, extending British influence, and circulating our language to the uttermost parts of the earth.

But to return to my subject, the invasion of India. It may well be assumed, as a probable consequence, that one of the greatest, richest, and most fertile countries in the world, should attract the attention, and excite the cupidity, of any ambitious power in Europe, whose object should be conquest and unlimited dominion, and, in the event of a general war, would be the prize for which a desperate game would be played. At present, we have nothing to fear. Any hostile attack on the side of Europe might be easily repulsed, so long as Persia and Turkey

remain even nominally independent, and the
Khans of the warlike tribes,—the Afghans,
Turkomans, Usbecks, Khelgees, Kyberees, Vi-
zeerees, &c., together with various others,
continue to remain attached to our interests.
Again, owing to the proximity of our eastern
empire with Persia, the Bengal government
could at any time, and without extraordinary
exertions, equip and dispatch an army of at
least 15,000 men; well appointed, and with the
usual complement of Europeans; this force, in
conjunction with the Persians, would be sufficient
(for it can hardly be supposed that nation is so
utterly lost to a sense of honour and independence as not to assist in the struggle,) to resist an
invading army, till a sufficient body of troops
could be collected to turn the balance in our
favour, should this have been previously doubtful.

We may naturally inquire how long we can
confide in the integrity of Persia as a friendly
neighbour, or how long she may be able to
maintain even the degree of independence she at
present possesses, with an imperious enemy
threatening her frontiers, and domineering in her
councils. For this contingency it is incumbent
on Great Britain to be prepared, and endeavour

to circumvent the machinations of the only
European or Asiatic power whose measures leave
no doubt upon the mind of any reasonable man
of the real nature of her intentions : already
feared by the neighbouring nations as the most
formidable combatant in the field of Asiatic warfare, her position and resources point her out as
the nation most likely to grasp at universal
dominion in Asia ; the very poverty of her
barren steppes would, even if no other motive
existed, excite her numerous hordes to invade
and possess themselves of more fertile countries.
Already mistress of the provinces to the north of
the Araxas, with the Euxine and Caspian Seas,
she appears—if we may judge from the settlements and forts lately erected on the eastern
banks of the Caspian, and from the circumstance
that agents have been openly despatched with
costly presents to the Khans of Bokhara, Khiva,
and Khojend — that the extensive and long
matured plans of aggression are about to assume
a character by which she will be able to reap the
real fruits of so much costly preparation ; facts
which have occasioned no inconsiderable sensa-
tion in Calcutta.

In addition to this, the young and inexperienced

Shah of Persia has been encouraged to invade
Herat, evidently for the purpose of wasting his
resources ; when this is effected, we shall see
Russia proceed to crush her victim in the same
manner as Catherine deposed the last Khan of
Krim Tartary. Let but a short time pass away,
and an army of Muscovites will be seen hastening to the assistance of its protegée, which will
have the effect of transferring the Russian frontier
from Arras to Herat !—and another of the dark
dramas of Russian policy will be represented, in
which she first caresses and then stabs her confiding victim.

Let any of my readers refer to the map, and
regard the position of Herat, and he will immediately perceive how practicable it would be for
a well-appointed European army to march from
thence to the banks of the Indus in forty days ;
the Kaffilahs have been known to make it in
twenty-five days.

We will suppose an invading army at Herat.
From this place to Cabool, which is within
twelve days' journey of the Indus, there are two
roads, the upper and the lower ; during winter the
latter, through Kandahar and Ghisnee, would
probably be preferred, and in summer the upper

could easily be traversed. From Cabool to Hindostan, through Peshawar, the route, though not altogether without difficulties, is practicable.

We cannot, of course, calculate upon the obstacles which the native tribes might interpose in the way of an invading army; for, owing to their semi-barbarous state and rude method of warfare, they would not be likely to avail themselves of the fastnesses of their country against disciplined European forces; but, relying on the known excellence of their swords and skill in using them, expose themselves to the danger of being cut off in great numbers. It is, however, possible they might pursue the same line of conduct they did on former occasions,—that is, join the army of the invader, and share in the spoil.

In addition to those through Persia, there are, I believe, four other routes which might be available for an army desirous to approach India from the Caspian Sea. The Emperor Paul's favourite plan of invasion was by way of Oorgunge,—the Russian government having made, or contemplating, an alliance with a formidable tribe of that name, and then intending to effect a passage through their territories to Bokhara, as it is said

there are fewer strong-holds or fortified positions
on this than on any other route. After passing
the river Amu, the invading army were then to
proceed to Balkh by way of Karjoo and Kirchee,
at which latter place they were to obtain a
sufficient stock of provisions, preparatory to
passing the Himalayah range of mountains; and,
as the attempt was to be made during the summer
months, the Hindoo-Cosh was selected as the
best road for a large army, the ascent being
gradual and less fatiguing. Provided they had
arrived thus far, it was presumed the principal
difficulties in this gigantic undertaking would
have been overcome; but Paul was not the man
to calculate the dangers and privations his troops
would have had to endure; the moral and physical obstacles they would have to overcome, in
contending with the diseases incidental to the
climate, in crossing the trackless deserts, in
encountering the hostile tribes that would ever
hang upon their march and dispute their passage
through every glen and defile. But if Russia
seriously contemplated an invasion of Hindostan
during the reign of Paul, how much easier might
that now be accomplished, when her influence
and the fame of her arms extends through Cen-

tral Asia to Herat and the country of the
Afghans; when her boundaries have already
crossed the Araxas; when the Caspian Sea has
become a passage exclusively for her fleets, and
the independence of the Caucasus is trembling
in the balance of war.

An examination of even the remote practica-
bility of invasion, and the consideration of the
best means to be employed for the prevention of
such an enterprise, ought to engage the attention
of every man interested in the preservation of
our Asiatic empire. We must be immediately
struck with the expediency and importance of
maintaining the independence of every country
lying between the Russian frontier and the Indus.
It must be also evident, that these countries,
destitute alike of moral courage or the physical
strength necessary to repel aggression, must
eventually succumb, unless directed by the councils, and supported by the influence, of England.

Nearly the whole of Central Asia is in a state
of disorganization; the different countries torn
by intestine broils; the various tribes carrying
on the most extensive predatory warfare with
each other. Some persons seem to regard this
state of things as offering one of the greatest

difficulties interposed between India and an invading army from Europe. Still, I cannot but think, that if English military officers were encouraged to enter the service of some of the most powerful among the Khans, and organize their troops *à la Européen,* great good might be effected. I would particularly instance the warlike Afghans, so long a prey to anarchy, and without a settled form of government; their friendship ought certainly to be preserved and their power strengthened.

Much has been already done by the agents of the East India Company, in extending British interests and influence. The most powerful among the Arab chiefs, the Imaum of Muscat, carries on an extensive commercial intercourse with the two presidencies of Bengal and Calcutta. We also number him among our most faithful allies; and from his well known character for ambition, we cannot doubt, that if properly supported, he would gladly, and at any time, if such a measure should be thought advisable, make a descent upon the southern provinces of Persia, where a strong and well defended boundary might be formed.

Accredited residents have also been established

at Bushire and Bassorah, who exercise extensive
influence in those countries bordering on the
Persian Gulph. Possessing, as we do, all these
advantages and many more, we should not, therefore, relax in our endeavours to extend that influence, and to accumulate the difficulties an invading army would have to surmount.

Above all, the line of Russian frontier should
be fixed; for every inch that power advances
towards India only tends to create alarm—to
occasion an enormous expenditure in employing
agents to circumvent her machinations, and in
maintaining a large army ever ready to repel an
attack. Even granting that no actual danger
should exist of an invasion on the part of Russia,
still her approaches must be checked; we have
experience and examples enough to prove that
she would be a dangerous neighbour, skilled, as
she is, in all the seductive arts of sowing discord
and spreading dissatisfaction, which, thus excited,
would be certain to break forth in revolt and
rebellion, while the disaffected would ever find in
her a protector to shelter them from the punishment they deserved.

CHAPTER VII.

Right of Russia to the Caucasus canvassed—Heroic resistance of the Circassians against Russian invasion—
Treaty of Adrianople—Conduct of Sultan Mahmoud
with respect to that treaty—Threats of the Russian
ambassador at Constantinople—Sefir Bey, the Circassian envoy—His expulsion from Constantinople—Observations upon the invasion of Circassia—Governor
Yermeloff—His tyrannical character—Admission of
Russian agents in the Caucasus that Circassia was independent.

AFTER this long digression upon the invasion
of India and its consequences, we shall return to
the subject of the Western Caucasus, and say a
few words on the pretensions of Russia to that
country. As a preliminary, I would invite the
attention of the reader to the description of my
voyage round the Black Sea, in my late work.
In relating the details of this, I have already
shewn that the contest in the Western Caucasus
is the struggle of a free independent people

against a foreign power, determined to enforce its unfounded claim by force of arms.

It will be seen that along the whole line of the Circassian coast there is not a single Russian settlement, with either custom-house or indeed with any establishment to shew that the natives have been at any time under the authority of Russia or Turkey; for, let it be remembered, if the Circassians are, as Russia pretends, revolted subjects, some traces would undoubtedly remain of their former rule; whereas, so far from this being the case, the few miserable forts of mud and palisadoes bear every mark of having been constructed (with the exception of Anapa) within these few years; to which we may add, that beyond their guns not a single Russian soldier dare advance, not even to procure water, unless accompanied with a park of artillery.

Finding she could not subjugate this warlike people by the repeated invasions which carried fire and sword into their mountain recesses, and wishing to conceal this political enormity from civilized Europe, the whole coast was strictly blockaded from the mouth of the Kouban to the Phase in Mingrelia. But notwithstanding the Russian pennant floated in every bay and creek,—

notwithstanding the Circassians almost daily witnessed the capture or destruction of their little barks, and those of their neighbours the Turks, who, actuated either by cupidity or sympathy, ventured on the daring attempt of eluding the Russian cruizers,—still they refused to submit. Even though shut out from every aid, pecuniary, moral, or military,—debarred from receiving the most essential necessaries of life—they have successfully maintained the unequal contest, destroyed the best disciplined troops of their invader, and carried their victorious arms into the very territory of their oppressor : a resistance, when we remember the magnitude of the force employed against them, and their own limited resources, (being too frequently, from the want of ammunition, obliged to have recourse to the arrow and the sword,) unequalled, perhaps, in the annals of any nation. Must we not therefore admit that this people, by their almost superhuman exertions, have been the principal check to Russian ambition in the East, in maintaining the independence of their country, which may be termed the key to Persia, Turkey, and India, and thereby rendered a valuable service, not only to England, but to Europe ?

It would be a futile attempt, even were I disposed to favour the views of the autocrat, to
point out one single passage in the history of
the Caucasus, or any article in the treaties
between Turkey and Russia, that could substan-
tiate his right of sovereignty to the Caucasus.
On the other hand, if my space and time would
allow me, I could recount a frightful catalogue of
the crimes, the intrigues, the barbarities, and the
bribery, his agents have employed, in endeavouring to obtain from this simple-minded people
permission to form commercial settlements on
their coasts.

The treaty of Adrianople,* which it is

---

* *Treaty of Adrianople*, Article IV.   Signed, September
the 14th, 1829.

Georgia, Imeritia, Gouriel, and several other provinces
of the Caucasus, (*plusieurs autres provinces du Caucase,*)
having been for many years, and in perpetuity, united to the
empire of Russia, and that empire having, besides, by the
treaty concluded with Persia at Tourkmantchai, on the 10th
of February, 1828, acquired the Khanats of Erivan and
Naktchiran, the two high contracting parties have recognised the necessity of establishing between their respective
states, on the whole of that line, a well-determined frontier,
capable of preventing all future discussion; they have equally
taken into consideration the *proper means to oppose insur-
mountable obstacles to the incursions and depredations which the*

notorious was negotiated in fraud, and enforced at the point of the bayonet, does not even mention Circassia. We see Turkey, in the fourth article of that treaty, is compelled to acknowledge the right of Russia to Georgia, Imeritia, Gouriel, and *several other provinces of the Caucasus;* a right deduced from the circumstance, that they

neighbouring nations or tribes hitherto committed, and which have so often compromised the relations of friendship and good feeling between the two empires; consequently, it has been agreed upon to consider henceforward, as the frontiers between the territories of the imperial court of Russia and those of the Sublime Porte in Asia, the line which, following the present limit of Gouriel from the Black Sea, ascends ascends as far as the border of Imeritia, and from thence in the straightest direction as far as the point where the frontiers of Akhaltzick and of Kars meet those of Georgia; leaving, in this manner, to the north of, and within, that line, the town of Akhaltzick and the fort of Khalnalick, at a distance of not less than two hours. All the countries situated to the south and west of this line of demarcation, towards the pachalicks of Kars and Trebizond, together with the major part of the pachalick of Akhaltzick, shall remain in perpetuity under the dominion of the Sublime Porte; whilst those which are situated to the north and east of the said line, towards Georgia, Imeritia, and Gouriel, *as well as all the littoral of the Black Sea, from the mouth of the Kouban, as far as the port of St. Nicholas, inclusively,* under the dominion of the Emperor of Russia.

had been for many years annexed to the Russian empire. By the same treaty, Turkey was obliged to establish a boundary line in strict conformity with the wishes of her conqueror, and to assign her the whole coast of the Black Sea, from the mouth of the Kouban, near Anapa, to Fort St. Nicholas, at the southern extremity of Gouriel. That is as much as to say, I (Turkey) assign whatever right or title I may have to Circassia, and promise that I will not interfere with you (Russia) in your endeavours to subdue it, in the same manner as the sovereign Pontiff of Rome, the spiritual chief of the Catholics, might dispose of his loving subjects in Ireland, to his most Catholic Majesty, Don Carlos ; the Sultan of Constantinople having no other authority in Circassia than that arising from being the spiritual head of the Mahomedan faith. For, with respect to the Circassian territory, Turkey never did possess a foot of land in that country, save and except the two insulated forts, Anapa and Souchom-Kalé, (Soudjouk-Kalé having been long since destroyed,) and these she only held, on sufferance from the natives, as commercial depots.

The real intentions of Russia will immediately appear from the perusal of this clever document,

which she purposely caused to be most ambigu-
ously framed, being fully aware that the *plusieurs
autres provinces du Caucase* were nearly unknown
to the people of Europe, or, at least, they entertained very vague notions respecting them. If
she had at that time invested Turkey with the
sovereignty of Circassia by name, it would have
awakened the jealousy of the European powers,
and have been regarded by them as a flagrant
violation of her own treaties, by which she had
stipulated not to seek for any increase of territory
or to grasp at any commercial advantages afforded
by the navigation of the Black Sea not attainable
by every other nation.

But no sooner is the jealousy of Europe lulled
to sleep than, all at once, we see Circassia invaded, its coasts openly blockaded, and the·inha-
bitants denounced as rebels to her authority, on
the plea of having derived the right to its sovereignty from her treaties with the Sublime Porte!
Still, notwithstanding all her endeavours to allay
the suspicion and blindfold the vigilance of diplo-
matists, this very document, were there no other
proof, establishes beyond doubt the fact that the
Circassians were an independent people, by
alluding to the " proper means to oppose insur-

mountable obstacles to the incursions and depredations which the neighbouring tribes had hitherto
committed." Now, if these neighbouring tribes
(the Circassians) were Turkish or Russian subjects, how could they have so often compromised
the harmony and good feeling between the two
empires ?

It is evident that the Sultan did not understand
the tendency of this document, or he would never
have been so unjust as to attempt to transfer a
country over which he had no authority beyond
that of being the spiritual chief of its inhabitants.
Indeed, I have every reason for believing, from the
information I received from my friends at Constantinople, and also from the subsequent conduct
of the Sultan relative to Circassia, that he felt the
full weight of the serious responsibility he had
incurred by even indirectly transferring a right to
the littoral of a country over which he knew he had
not the slightest control. His consciousness of this,
and of the train of evils which he had thus unknow-
ingly inflicted upon a country it was his interest
to uphold, and to whose people he was united by
the dearest ties of consanguinity, was frequently
exhibited in the most violent bursts of indignation ; but, on discovering the real extent of the

duplicity practised upon him by the court of St. Petersburg, he was known (if report speaks true) to have threatened repeatedly to proclaim to Europe that Circassia was independent, unless the Russian government should consent to abrogate that part of the treaty relating to the littoral of the Black Sea.

It must therefore be evident, if the ambassadors of the leading powers of Europe, by interest opposed to Russia, had taken advantage of the ferment at that time in Constantinople, when both Sultan and people were so highly incensed against the enemy that had so often deceived and triumphed over them, Circassia might have been saved all the horrors of a murderous war, and a barrier placed against any further encroachments of Russia in the east, while England would have been spared the humiliation of seeing her national flag insulted.

The illustrious victim of Russian intrigue, finding that he met with no sympathy from the European powers, and conscious of the feeble state of his empire and his very limited resources, was obliged to submit to the imperious remonstrances of his powerful enemy.

It is, however, but justice to the character of

the Sultan to say, that he still continued to assist
the Circassians with his councils, if not with more
substantial aid.   Gifts and honours were publicly
lavished upon the distinguished chieftain, Sefir
Bey, the accredited envoy from the confederated
princes of Circassia to the Ottoman Porte.   In
addition to this, every class, age, and sex, manifested the warmest interest in the cause of the
Circassians, and celebrated their victories with
undisguised satisfaction.

At these open demonstrations of sympathy on
the part of the Sultan and his people, the cabinet
of St. Petersburg instantly took the alarm; instructions were transmitted to their representative, M. Boutineff, to announce to the Turkish
government that either he or the obnoxious Sefir
Bey must quit Constantinople.   As may be supposed, the remonstrances of a sovereign supported
by a million of bayonets prevailed, for the hapless
stranger was transported into the interior of Rou-
melia.

Thus the Ottoman Porte, with its humiliated
sovereign, is obliged to accede unresistingly to
every demand of Russia, whether just or unjust;
thus she is obliged to refuse atonement to an injured people for an unintentional error, in having,

through ignorance of the precise geographical
limits of the countries forming the subject of the
treaty, disposed of a territory which did not belong
to her, either de jure or de facto. Vain, however,
will be every endeavour of the court of St. Petersburg to extinguish the burning desire for revenge
which glows in the breast of the Turkish sovereign and his people, and which, like a pent-up
volcano, will burst forth on the first fitting occasion.

After all that has been already said respecting
the right of Russia to the sovereignty of Circassia,
it would be useless to enter into any further discussion on this subject. I would, however, refer
those among my readers who may be interested
in a more detailed account of the aggressive policy of Russia in the Caucasus, to that interesting
work, "Progress of Russia in the East. 1836."

Even granting that no other ground existed on
which to establish the independence of Circassia,
the very fact of the inhabitants having maintained
themselves against the whole force of Russia since
the treaty of Adrianople, in 1829, would alone be
sufficient for this purpose, according to the opinions of all public jurists who admit of a seven
years' hostility, it being considered that if no de-

finite period were fixed when the struggle between
the oppressed and the oppressor must of necessity
terminate, that strife and bloodshed would never
cease to agitate the nations.

In every shape we must view the attempt of
Russia to subdue the Caucasus as the crusade
of might against right, and entirely at variance
with the laws of civilized nations ; and as to the
pretence of a sovereignty derived from the Sublime Porte, that is one of the grossest fabrications
ever invented, and which must entail indelible
disgrace upon the Russian government,—a disgrace which history will most assuredly perpe-
tuate to posterity.   Indeed, if I were disposed to
pursue this subject to any length, it would not
be difficult, according to national law, and the
dictates of strict justice, to dispute her right even
to the provinces she already holds on the coast of
the Black Sea—the Crimea, Mingrelia, Imeritia,
and Gouriel, all of which have been obtained by
the most consummate and persevering intrigue.
But granting that she may be able to bring forward the semblance of a claim to those countries,
she cannot even prove the shadow of a pretension
to Circassia, for, as I before observed, the two
settlements possessed by Turkey on the Circas-

sian coast were mere commercial depots, no Turk
or other trader daring to penetrate into the interior of the country unless protected by a konak
(Circassian chieftain) ; and so far from the people
paying tribute or rendering homage to the Porte,
that power was obliged to expend large sums
annually for the purpose of maintaining a friendly
intercourse with the mountaineers, with those
hardy warriors whom she regarded as the best
protection against the further aggrandizement of
Russia. Besides, in all the marauding expeditions of the Circassians into the territories of
Russia, and the hostilities of that power against
Circassia during the last fifty years, let it be remembered, that neither of these powers ever remonstrated with the other, which would not have
been the case were the Circassians vassals of the
Sublime Porte. Neither would humanity have
been outraged with the recital of the barbarities
committed by the Russian general, the tyrant
Yermoloff, upon the unconquerable children of the
Caucasus,—it being the duty (were there no other
motive than cupidity) of every government, however uncivilized, to succour its subjects from the
desolating brand of the invader. Again, we have
only to turn to the treaties of Russia with the

Ottoman Porte, the travels of the Russian agents, Messieurs Güldenstadt, Pallas, and Klaproth, the instructions of the government of St. Petersburg to its generals in the Caucasus,—all of which tend to confirm that the inhabitants were independent either of Turkish or Russian authority.

Klaproth, who visited the Caucasus in 1807, in his advice to the Russian government as to the most practicable method of subjugating Circassia, in Chapter XXII. of his Travels, says—

" It is absolutely necessary that the government (Russian), for the safety of its provinces,—Mingrelia, Imeritia, and Gouriel, as well as the country of the Tchernemorsky Cossacks,—should secure the whole coast of the Black Sea, from Anapa to Poti in Mingrelia. It is also expedient to endeavour to keep on good terms with the princes and elders of the Abasian tribes on the coast of the Black Sea, on account of the powerful influence they exercise over their neighbours, and the strong situation they inhabit. In order to conciliate their friendship, nothing more is necessary than to present them annually with a few cart-loads of salt, an article of which they are entirely destitute, and so necessary to the preservation of their flocks and herds.

" The government should also attempt to retain one prince or chieftain, at least, of every
tribe in its interest; this may probably be
effected by flattery and bribery.

" The Tchernemorsky Cossacks, on the other
side of the Kouban, should be peremptorily for-
bidden to sell salt to the Circassians. The government only should dispose of it, to such princes
and elders of tribes as may have submitted to its
authority."

Events have proved how implicitly this advice
has been followed.

In Chapter XXIX., when speaking of the new
military road, the Wladi Kaukas, leading from
the Russian territories across the Caucasus to
Georgia, he says,—" If this fortress, the Wladi
Kaukas, (which has given its name to this military road,) being the key to the Caucasus in
this quarter, were better regulated, it would
become a place of great importance. In fact,
there is but one method of securing the territories of Russia on this side of the Terek, and
that is, to endeavour by every means possible to
dissolve the *commercial connexion* between the
inhabitants of the Caucasus and the Turks.

" For the accomplishment of this object, the

following plan might be adopted :—let a military cordon be established along the Kouban from the redoubt of Nedremannoi to the stone bridge which crosses that river; let forts be erected upon it, which might be kept up without any great expense : if they were also made to serve the purposes of salt magazines, the tribes residing beyond the Kouban might purchase this article at the rate of one rouble sixty kopecks per pud. By means of this cordon, if efficiently guarded, all communication between the Kabardians and those Circassian tribes living in the neighbourhood of the Black Sea would be completely cut off, while the former could no longer receive and secure the plunder taken upon the line. They would also have more difficulties to surmount when making incursions into the Russian territory; while, at the same time, it would be impossible for them to transport their Russian prisoners to the coast of the Black Sea, to be disposed of to the Turkish traders."

CHAPTER VIII.

Excursion on the banks of the Schaukwassa river—Aspect
of the country—The Tubi and the Ubick—Their
singular appearance—Character for fierceness—Weapons
—Description of the Kara-Kalkan tribe—The Demirghoi—Their fortifications—System of agriculture—Cultivation of the vine—Bees—Pastoral habits of the
people—Primitive mills—Treacherous conduct of Russia
towards the inhabitants of the Western Caucasus.

HAVING now as it were paved the way to the
continuation of my tour in the Caucasus, and
in some degree familiarized the reader with the
moral, social, and political state of the inhabitants, I will resume my narrative.

After spending a few days with the Demirghoi
chieftain Aitek Tcherei, or *Inal Tschantemeer*,
(the iron-hearted prince,) a name bestowed upon
him by his followers on account of his obduracy
in not granting quarter to his enemies in the field,
we continued our route along the banks of the

Schaukwassa, or, as the Tartars call it, Schauk-etscheck, a considerable river, which has its source in that part of the alps called the Snowy Mountains, near Mount Schagalish. The left bank, high and rocky, with few exceptions, is quite impassable, even to the fearless Circassian and his sure-footed steed; while the right bank, less abrupt, presented at intervals a prospect beautifully undulating; however, from the serpentine direction in which it traversed the country, and the frequent obstructions of jutting rocks, together with the narrowness of the valley, we were obliged to ford it several times, not however without becoming more intimately acquainted with its cooling freshness than was agreeable during an autumnal excursion in the mountains.

The water of the Schaukwassa is clear, the current for the most part rapid, and abounds with fish ; and the finest forest trees everywhere skirt its banks, among which the oak and the valona seemed to rear their proud heads almost to an altitude with the lofty hills. This river and the Laba rank among the principal of the second-rate rivers in the Western Caucasus. Several tributary streams flow into it, and, after running through a country generally speaking highly favourable to agriculture and grazing, empties itself into the Kouban nearly opposite the Russian redoubt Plastimiwurskoi, situated on the right bank of that river.

The neighbourhood of the more elevated part of the Schaukwassa river, near its source, and in the high mountain ridge that extends towards Ghelendjik and Pchad, is the home perhaps of the fiercest of all the Caucasian races, called the Tubi and the Ubick, who, with their allies, the Adami, the Muchosch, and the Demirghoi, can muster at least a body of seven thousand men capable of bearing arms. The Russians have never been able to penetrate in this direction beyond the village of Minbulatia, about twenty wersts from the Kouban, which they burned last year.

We met a body of about five hundred of these Tubians and Ubickians, who had come down from their strongholds to assist their brethren, the Demirghoi, (whose chief they acknowledge in time of war as their leader,) in the approaching struggle. They were all on foot, (unusual for a Circassian,) owing to the inaccessible nature of their mountain home, which affords very unsafe

footing for horses ; or, if I might credit the accounts I received, for any other animals save goats
and these chamois-like men. They were nearly all
of gigantic height, and their countenances rather
prepossessing than otherwise, except that the
expression was fierce even to wildness, which
was not a little increased by their head-dress,
consisting of a white sheepskin turban, the wool
of which, being unusually long, curled over their
face and shoulders. They were attired in the
usual tunic of the Circassians ; over this they
wore the tchaouka,—a black mantle, made from
goat's hair and sheep's wool plaited together,
which altogether added not a little to the ferocity of their appearance. Sandals of untanned
leather or the bark of the linden tree was the
only covering for the feet.

Every man was well armed, from the poniard
and hatchet in his belt to the light gun slung
across his shoulder. In addition to these,
each of them carried a club that might have
served Herculus ; at least, it appeared to be of
sufficient weight and dimensions to have felled
an ox ; for, to say nothing of its being knotty, it
was furnished at one end with a steel barb a
foot in length. This ponderous javelin during

their journey served to assist them in springing
over rivers and from cliff to cliff,—also as a rest
for their gun, to take more deadly aim,—and,
during their hours of amusement, as a toy to
hurl at a mark, a feat which they performed with
the most fearful exactness. They expressed the
utmost impatience to be led against the enemy,
the hated Urus—a name, in the phraseology of
the Attéghéi tribes, for the Russians; and I must
confess, when I contemplated these half-savage
mountaineers, I thought their appearance alone
sufficient to scare an army of Russian soldiers.

We also met with another tribe of ferocious-
looking mountaineers, on their march to the
camp of the Demirghoi chieftain, from the upper
regions of the black mountains, called by their
neighbours Kara-Kalkan, from the circumstance
of their using black shields on the field of battle.
Their dress and weapons were similar to those of
the Tubi, except that each man carried his
shield, made of wood, and covered with the hide
of a buffalo; this was strengthened by bands of
iron or yew. Being deficient in ammunition,
numbers were armed with bows and arrows,
besides the light gun.

The following sketch will give the reader some

idea of the costume of these people, and the form
of their weapons :—

The inhabitants of this part of the high lands
in the province of Demirghoi, or, as they pronounce it in their own dialect, Kemirquahee,
fortify their villages with great care; but however available these defences might be against
an attack of their predatory countrymen, merely
armed with rifles, bows, and arrows, they would
not stand even a slight shock of the European
howitzer. These primitive fortifications consist
of a double paling of about seven feet high, and
four feet distant from each other; between

them is an earth entrenchment, which fills the
intermediate space, except in those places left
for loop-holes. The paling forming the inner
enclosure is usually covered with straw or reeds,
and within this we find stables for the cattle and
sheds for the agricultural implements. The
only preparations for defence made by these
simple people consist of the loop-holes from
which to fire on the enemy, and most primitive
watch-towers, like those of the Cossacks:
although these are nothing more than four poles
fastened in the earth, their height, twenty feet,
enables the Circassian to descry a distant enemy,
when he fires a torch to alarm his countrymen.
The entrance to the enclosure, which is very
narrow, is barricadoed with carts and logs of
timber.

Agriculture seemed to be almost entirely neg-
lected in this part of the Western Caucasus, with
the exception of sowing a little barley and millet,
the favourite grain of these people ; at the same
time, the land was, in most places, so rich as
scarcely to require any tillage. When they fix
upon a spot they intend to cultivate, they
merely set fire to the long grass and brushwood,
which serves at once as an easy method of clear-

ing the land and nourishing it. The most
abundant crops soon follow. After these have
been harvested, the ground is frequently left to
run wild for a year or two, when they renew the
same process.

The various agricultural operations are performed by the aid of oxen, while mules and
asses are employed as beasts of burden,—the
Circassians considering it derogatory to the dignity of the horse to degrade him by any other
labour more fatiguing than that of the saddle.
The vine is not a stranger to the sunny slopes of
the hills ; and the wine would really be excellent,
were it not for the unpleasant flavour it receives
from the skins in which they keep it, the inside of them being pitched.

The whole of the Circassian tribes appear to
have a universal passion for the rearing of bees ;
this insect being regarded with the most superstitious veneration, no family, however poor,
is without several hives. Mead is one of
their favourite drinks, and honey an article
of the first necessity in the cuisine. Such, indeed, is the general popularity of bees, that a
Circassian family deem themselves fortunate in
proportion to the number of hives they possess,

and consider the multiplication of these insects as a harbinger of prosperity.

The Demirghoi tribes, from the number of their flocks and herds, may be termed, when compared with their brethren on the Black Sea, a wealthy people, and are perfectly pastoral in their habits ; indeed, they are fortunate in the country they possess, when we remember its mountainous character. Abundance of the finest trees adorn the sides of their hills ; the plateaus on the mountains form excellent grazing land ; and on the banks of the numerous brooks and springs we find the finest meadows, which might be made still more luxuriant and extensive if irrigation were more generally introduced.

They roam with their flocks and herds from dale to dale, from hill to hill. This does not arise from the necessity of providing herbage, but from the constant apprehension of a visit from their neighbours, the Cossacks and Russians ; consequently, they always hold themselves, and their flocks and herds, prepared to make a journey at a moment's notice.

Wherever the nature of the country is such as to render the transportation of cannon (the only weapon dreaded by the Circassians) impossible, they live in permanent villages, dividing their time between war, the chase, and the cares of the herdsman. Temperate in their manner of living, the dairy and bees supply their choicest food, and their bread consists of small barley cakes, baked upon a hot stone or iron plate, covered with hot cinders.

Besides the rivers and rivulets, the country everywhere abounds with tiny brooks and springs, which offer the facility of erecting water mills; consequently, we find one attached to every hamlet and farm-house, which, though simple in construction, is well adapted to the purpose for which it is required. The mill-stone is set in motion by a small horizontal wheel, against which the water is discharged through the trunk of a hollow tree. A hopper, in the shape of a funnel, and made from the bark of some tree, is suspended by willow ropes, and a sharp-pointed stone, moving in the cavity of another, answers the purpose of an iron pintle to the axle-tree. These mills, like everything else useful or valuable in this ill-fated country, are so constructed as to admit of being transported; consequently, an enemy when invading the country finds it to be a desert, without provisions for themselves, or the

slightest forage, beyond what they can glean on
the mountains, for their cattle. Even the villages are frequently in flames, it being a common
practice for the inhabitants to set them on fire
when they retreat to more inaccessible situations.

Can we, then, feel surprised at the deadly
hatred these people entertain towards the Russians, who commenced their intercourse (a fact
admitted in the writings of their own agents,
Pallas, Klaproth, and others) under the mask of
proffered protection, friendly commerce, and a
desire to instruct them in the civilizing truths of
Christianity; instead of which the wily Muscovite gradually encroached upon the Circassian
territory, until the unlucky natives are now cooped
up in its mountain fastnesses, and, last of all,
the finest youths of the country have been kid-
napped to swell the hosts of the imperial autocrat
at St. Petersburg, and astonish the world by their
dexterity in horsemanship, and in throwing the
djerrid.

The rich undulating pastures, down to the
morasses near the Kouban, have become to the
mountaineers utterly useless, except during a
month or two in winter, on account of the facilities that part of their territory affords to the

enemy to attack them with their artillery. These
once fertile meadows are now a mere desert, the
abode of the wild boar and the pelican, the Russians themselves being unable to colonize them
on account of the unceasing hostility of the natives.

CHAPTER IX.

Caucasian rivers—Marshes of the Kouban—Game—Wild
boars—Distant prospect of the fortress of Anapa—Account of that fortress—Return to the camp of the confederated chiefs on the banks of the Ubin—Description of the rivers in the vicinity—The Elberous—
Definition of its name in the Caucasian dialects—Black
mountains—Inaccessible nature of the country—Similarity between the ancient Swiss and the mountaineers of
the Caucasus.

On leaving the Schaukwassa, we took a south-
westerly direction towards Anapa and Soudjouk-
Kalé. In the course of our excursions we crossed
several rivers of secondary importance, and rivulets, the whole of which were at this time, in
some places at least, fordable. Judging, however, from the width of the bed, and various indications on their banks, such as broken trees and
logs of timber, there could be no doubt that they
are much swollen in spring, after the snow has
melted in the mountains.

The most considerable among these rivers, the Aphibs of the Circassians, and the Kara Kouban of the Tartars and Russians, has its source in the great Caucasian range, called by the Circassians Kurdtsh, (snowy mountains.) After receiving several small tributary streams, it flows into the main river, the Kouban, about fifteen miles lower down than the Schaukwassa.

From the mouth of this river commences the extensive marshes of the Kouban, which continue on to the liman of the Black Sea, forming one of the most unhealthy districts perhaps in the world. How often have the unfortunate Russian soldiers, bowed down by sickness and a harassing war, found an untimely grave in this pestilential marsh! The reeds and sedges frequently attain the height of twelve feet, affording shelter not only to vast numbers of water-fowl of every species, but to the wild boars, which haunt it in great numbers. These animals are famous for their ferocity and great size. During the winter months, when the Russians retire within their intrenchments, they afford capital sport to the mountaineers, who usually hunt them down with dog and spear.

After passing the Otaschalgan, inferior in size and volume of water to the Aphibs, we again entered the country of the Nottakhaitzi tribes. This river is called, by the Tartars and Russians, Jamansu, (noxious water,) on account of the water being generally turbid and impregnated with mineral ; it falls into the Kouban about eight miles lower down than the Aphibs.

A few miles further, commences the very extensive province of the Khapsoukhie,* or, the Schapschick of the Russians, separated from that of the Nottakhaitzi, or Natuchaskee of the Russians, by the small river Attakum, which, soon swelled by numerous springs and rivulets, divides in two branches ; the one joins the waters of the Aphibs, and the other meanders down to the marshes, and from thence to the liman of the Black Sea.

From the heights above this river we caught a splendid view of the Kouban and its extensive marshes, with the redouts, stanitzas, and fortresses of the Tchernemorsky cossacks on the opposite side of the river ; the long ridge of hills that skirt the coast from Anapa to Soudjouk-Kalé ; while,

* As we shall have occasion to refer to this province frequently in the course of our narrative, we shall, in order to avoid vagueness, designate it for the future by the name Khapsoukhie.

in the far distance, the Euxine glittered in the
sun like a sheet of crystal, and the town and fortress of Anapa, with the Russian camp, gave
picturesque effect and animation to the vast landscape.

We could not have been many miles distant
from Anapa, for I could distinctly discern with
my glass the preparations of the military in the
camp for the approaching struggle ; pack-horses,
mules, and camels, were in the act of being loaded
with provisions and ammunition ; cossacks were
galloping to and from the fort, and the infantry
were forming into lines.

According to the account of the Circassians,
the fortress of Anapa was built by the Turks, about
fifty years ago. The fort stands on a projecting
eminence of the Kitzilkaya mountains, which
here abruptly terminates in a dead plain of about a
mile and a half in extent to the sea coast, where
it is surrounded by a fortification consisting of a
wall and ditch defended by bastions ; to the south
and south-west the fort and town is overhung by
an encircling chain of almost perpendicular rocks,
rising to a height of from one to two hundred feet, forming a natural and effectual defence
against the attacks of the mountaineers, who are

as yet unprovided with any other weapon more effective against fortified positions than the musket; however, as they still hold possession of the whole of the adjoining hills, the inhabitants of the fort and town are completely hemmed in, except towards the sea and the north, in which direction, the country being flat and marshy, they are enabled to hold communication with the Tchernemorsky cossacks on the right banks of the Kouban; but they are deprived even of this resource when the Kouban inundates the neighbouring country, which is generally the case in the spring, when the snow has melted in the mountains, and in the autumn, after a succession of heavy rains, which usually fall about that time.

Since the warfare has assumed a more deadly character, the inhabitants of the town and the garrison have suffered the severest privations, particularly from the want of sufficient water, there being only one well in the town, and that highly insalubrious, which obliges the garrison to fetch water from a neighbouring spring in the hills, accompanied by cannon with lighted matches: notwithstanding this precaution, such is the daring hostility of the mountaineers, that the expeditions to procure water are generally attended with loss of life.

But to resume the account of my journey. After a tiresome ride of eight days, we again entered the grand camp, where the confederated princes and chiefs of Circassia, with thousands of their followers, had assembled on the banks of the Ubin. This little river, as also the Aschips, the Ill, the Baken, and the Zemes, runs through some of the strongest gorges in this part of the Caucasus; the Bakan flows in the direction of Anapa, where, at the extremity of the defile of the same name, it unites with the Attakum above described; the Zemes (in Russian, Doba,) falls into the bay of Soudjouk-Kalé, while the others, in summer, are mere rivulets, and only contribute to swell the marshes of the Kouban.

The whole of these small rivers take their rise in the upper regions of the Black Mountains, some of the lower ranges of which we had recently traversed. They are called by the Circassians, Kuschhaa, and by the Russians Teherne-gori, (Black Mountains,) from the circumstance of being densely covered with foliage, and to distinguish them from the more elevated range covered with eternal snow, of which the Elberous forms the highest pinnacle. Elberous, however, is not the proper name for that far-famed alp, this being the general appellation given by the Caucasians to all elevated summits where winter ever reigns, so that a traveller in the Caucasus, in search of the Elberous, *would find that alp multiplied perhaps to a hundred.* The proper name by which it is known to the Circassians is, Osha Makhua, (Mountain of Happiness,) and to the neighbouring tribes in Upper Abasia, the Orfeeif-Gubb, the Heavenly Mountain, or the Mountain of the Great Spirit; while the Tartars give it the very expressive name, Ildis-Thaglar, (Mountain of Stars.) The whole of these tribes consider it as the residence of Tschin Padishah, the mighty emperor of the furies and other aerial spirits, to whom they have been accustomed to fly for support in case of their being unfortunate in war.

The whole of the country over which I had lately passed, and that by which I was now surrounded, was beautifully picturesque, and, making allowance for its mountainous nature, well adapted to agricultural purposes; for, although most of the dales, gorges, and defiles, are narrow, and generally overhung with limestone rocks of no great elevation, there are abundance of detached spots of fertile land, together with the verdant plateaus, capable of nourishing a numerous population; and, if we may judge from the frequent

occurrence of villages and hamlets, the number of children, and particularly when we remember the protracted war, we must consider
the population to be on the increase since the
dreadful visitation of the plague in 1812, which
swept away the inhabitants of whole districts.

This stupendous range of the Black Mountains, instead of presenting one continuous line,
is rent and broken into numerous chasms and
ridges, stretching north-west towards Anapa and
the Russian territory on the other side of the Kouban, and south-west in the direction of Ghelendjik
and Soudjouk-Kalé, forming gorges and defiles
for the most part perfectly inaccessible to an
enemy, as they not only contain no road, but the
inequalities and rugged nature of the country
render it impossible for any European army,
however enterprising, to transport the *materiel*
necessary to carry on a war with any probability
of a successful issue. Besides, they would have
to contend with a people who value liberty as
the greatest earthly good, and whose vigilance is
ever watching an opportunity to annihilate their
invaders.

Russia may appropriate the Black Sea ; she may
build forts on the coast ; she may prohibit the Cir-

cassians from receiving gunpowder and salt, the only articles they now stand in need of; but she cannot prevent them from fabricating these articles, having the materials at hand in their own mountains: salt springs are common in Upper Abasia; and their gunpowder, which I have given their method of manufacturing in my preceding volumes, is excellent. Consequently, I think we may infer that Russia will never be able effectually to subdue these mountaineers, a people so different from Europeans in general, who, independent of the most indomitable bravery, and the locality of their country, which operate strongly in their favour, are rendered still more formidable by their temperance, hardy habits, and contempt of danger.

Even the honest rugged Swiss, in the first dawn of their freedom, never worshipped the god of Liberty with greater devotion, never more gallantly defended their humble hearths. Wealth, honours, bribery, flattery, in short, all the cajoling influence of the intriguing court of St. Petersburg, have failed to corrupt them. Several of the princes and nobles have been exposed to all the fascinations of that polished court: they have been pensioned, elevated

to the highest military rank ; but, amidst all this
splendour, they have sighed after their mountain
home, to which they rarely fail to return.

Among many others, we may mention, as the
most celebrated, the two Kabardian chiefs, Ismael
and Bulat Atashuka.   Ismael served in the
Russian army with such distinction that he rose
to the rank of Major-General; and the Emperor
Alexander not only conferred upon him the
order of St. George, but, wishing to attach him
to his person and interests, loaded him with
favours : no temptation, however, could win him
permanently to adopt the manners of civilized
life, for he returned to his native mountains, to
enjoy his barley cakes and *skhou*, and the freedom
of roving over the woods and mountains, in pursuit of his favourite amusement, the chace.

The case of Bulat was even still more remarkable ; he was carried to St. Petersburg when little
more than an infant, where he was placed at the
military school, in which he acquired the French,
Italian, and Russian languages, so that he almost
forgot his own.   He was made an officer of
dragoons, and rose in a short time to the rank of
captain ; the same temptations of wealth and honours assailed his attachment to his native home,

but every allurement failed, and he returned to Circassia, where he now resides, on the banks of the Baksan, in one of the most secluded districts of Kabardia, as complete a mountain chief, — as determined a supporter of his country's independence, as the wildest hunter of the woods; and not all the solicitations, not all the promises of the emperor, could prevail upon him to send one of his children to be educated in Russia.

The Abasian prince, M. Scharavaschedze, a colonel in the Russian army, pursued a similar line of conduct. Last year, when we visited Bombora, in the neighbourhood of which he resides, the Governor General expected to have been welcomed by the prince, but he was disappointed, and thus I lost the opportunity of seeing courtly manners engrafted on mountain independence. The fact is, the Caucasians, one and all, detest the Russian yoke, and, indeed, we should suppose, from their peculiar habits and customs, that of any other foreign nation ; and, from being unaccustomed to restraint in their own country, military service in Russia they regard in no other light than ignominious slavery.

CHAPTER X.

Description of the country in the immediate vicinity of the
Russian fort Anapa—Ghelendjik and the Aboon—Preparation of the mountaineers for the expected attack of
the Russians—Anticipated success of the Circassians—
Projected plan of the Russian Government for the conquest of the Western Caucasus—General Willemineff—
His character and death.

THE camp on the Ubin, at which we were now
residing, and that on the Schaukwassa, before
alluded to, were not, however, the only military
stations of the mountaineers in this part of the
Caucasus ; for in addition to these were several
others of more or less importance, particularly
that in the defile of Baken, leading towards Anapa,
and the Zemes to Soudjouk-Kalé, while every
approach to the forts of Aboon and Nicholæfsky,
lately erected by General Wellemineff, some few
miles distant in the mountains, was strictly
guarded.

The whole of the heights and commanding positions were also occupied by sentinels, anxiously watching the movements of the enemy, each man being furnished with a torch of some combustible material, ready for ignition on the appearance of any part of the invaders.

This devoted district of the Western Caucasus, which had been, and was again to become, the theatre of so much bloodshed, is, in a manner, fenced in with Russian forts, consisting of Anapa and Ghelendjik on the Black Sea, the recent encampment at Soudjouk-Kalé, the redoubts, stanitzas, and fortresses, of the Tchernemorsky Cossacks on the right bank of the Kouban, together with the forts of Aboon and Nicholæfsky in the mountains.

Notwithstanding, however, the advantages the Russians possessed,—fortified positions, a fleet under Admiral Pallinotti, at their command, numbers, discipline, and the *materiel* of war,— they have been beaten back to their intrenchments, with great loss, in every attempt, since the commencement of the campaign, to penetrate into the interior. Encouraged by repeated successes, the enthusiasm of the mountaineers was highly excited, more especially as

they had received intelligence that their allies,
the Ingushes, the Ossetinians, and other tribes
that inhabit the great Caucasian range contiguous
to the Wladi Kaukas, together with the Lesghians
on the Caspian sea, had flown to arms, and
gained several signal triumphs over their common
enemy, having more than once surprised and
cut to pieces whole detachments from the grand
army in Georgia.

Hence the struggle which, only a few years
since, was principally confined to the provinces
on the Kouban and the Black Sea, now extends
throughout the whole Caucasus; and should the
same spirit of resistance once manifest itself
among the more peaceable inhabitants of Georgia,
Mingrelia, Imeritia, and Gourial, Russia may,
notwithstanding all her triumphs in the East, have
bitter cause to regret the war in Circassia; at all
events, this contest promises to give that power
more trouble, and to prove a greater drain, both
of men and treasure, than her expeditions against
the enfeebled monarchs of Turkey and Persia.

Whether this combination of the half civilized
inhabitants of the Caucasus will ultimately tend
to establish their independence, is a subject of
much speculation in the East. There is, how-

ever, every probability of success, if they continue to observe that unity of purpose and unanimity of action so lately introduced among them by a friendly stranger, Daoud Bey, and hitherto so foreign to their councils,—when, in consequence of their eternal feuds, tribe preyed upon tribe, and prince massacred prince. It should also be remembered, that disunion, bribery, and demoralization, the great allies and agents of Russia in her march to conquest, have here completely failed.

It cannot either be expected, even should that gallantry which in every age distinguished the chivalrous sons of Europe be extinct in our days, that their neighbours, the Turks and Persians, who must from political motives sympathize with the Caucasians, will long remain neutral spectators of a struggle in which their own interests are so deeply involved. Neither can we believe, that any Christian power will continue to protract a contest which must end in the extermination of a noble, a gallant people, who, we are persuaded, will never submit to a power they have learned to execrate from the cradle. To the best interests of Russia herself, if she persist in her aggression upon the liberties of a free people, the consequences of victory or defeat may be fatal. In the one case, the inhabitants of Europe, indignant at the outrage, and for their own interests alarmed at her formidable accession of power, may be roused to action, and call her to a dreadful account; while in the other, if the numerous tribes of the Caucasus persevere in their league of friendship, and pour forth their undisciplined hordes, her southern provinces may again, as of old, be entirely laid waste. The same spirit, the same determined purpose, animates the same people, that, in the same cause of fatherland and independence, placed a barrier against the great Macedonian conqueror,—repulsed and dispersed the valiant legions of immortal Rome, the well-trained bands of Mithridatesin,—after ages successively defeated every attempt of the Turks and Persians, in their most glorious days, to subdue them; and now keeps at bay the power that so often triumphed over Turkey and Persia, conquered Poland, and exterminated, or drove into exile, her bravest sons;—a semi-barbarous people, only known to Europe by the war that develops their real character, and, as it were, proclaims their existence.

What, then, might not an army achieve, and how disastrous their depredations, composed of such men, who, though unacquainted with the tactics of Europe, their very enemies, the Rus-

sians, acknowledge to be the finest cavalry soldiers in the world, whose glory is war, whose
profession is pillage, and whose revengeful spirit
is excited and encouraged by the fearful cry
which now resounds throughout the Caucasus—
"Avenge the death of our ancestors! The
fathers of our enemies shed the blood of our
fathers ; we will shed the blood of their children,
and exterminate their race! They have torn
from us our wives and our little ones ; they have
burned our villages, destroyed our flocks and
herds, and devastated our lands! The hour of
retribution is come!"—a people who never go
forth to battle without chanting in chorus a
defiance to their enemy. The following may
give the reader some idea of one of these popular
songs :—

> Hark! hark! the bugle's sounding!
> Away, to the hills away ;
> O'er peak and crag light bounding,
> As deer at break of day.
>
> We'll forth to slay the foe :
> Detested *Urus*,* die!
> Let vengeance deal the blow—
> Let ball and arrow fly.

* The Russians.

Loud booms the cannon's crash,
 The drums and trumpets sound,
Contending sabres clash,
 Through rocks and hills around.

We fight for those we love,
 For liberty and life;
Tkha-ah! * who reigns above,
 Protect us in the strife.

The setting sun shall fling
 O'er the sea its gory red;
Ere its latest beam takes wing,
 'Twill shine on Urus' dead.

Avenge, avenge our death!
 Sounds from our fathers' tomb;
Curs'd by their parting breath,
 Take, Urus, take thy doom!

Shades of our sires, behold,
 The vulture has its prey;
Let Heaven and earth behold—
 We've won, we've won the day!

The attempt to subdue this district of the
Western Caucasus was the result of a plan made
at St. Petersburg in 1834, and confided to the
execution of General Willemineff, who commenced
operations in the May of the following year, with
an army of twenty thousand men.   That gallant

---

* The Lord of Lords.

officer regarded the enterprise of such easy accomplishment, that he expressed his expectation of being able, in two summer campaigns, to subjugate the whole of the tribes from Anapa to Mingrelia.

Notwithstanding these confident anticipations of success, he utterly failed in making any permanent impression on the country, with the exception of the two isolated forts I before mentioned, which must be abandoned unless the hostile tribes in the vicinity are speedily subdued, owing to the fearful loss of life they entail in supplying them with provisions, and their uselessness as an effective check against the mountaineers.

"Year after year," says a young friend, who had served as a volunteer under General Willemineff, "the finest troops of this brave soldier were cut to pieces : perseverance, courage, foresight, military talent, availed him not, when opposed to the will of an entire people determined to be free; till at length, wearied with repeated reverses, he retired on the plea of ill health, and soon after died, in the flower of manhood, most probably a victim to that sickness of the spirit which corrodes the springs of existence.

Peace to his memory! He was a brave soldier, an excellent man ;—noble, generous, and open-hearted, he was beloved by his men, and respected by all who knew him.

" In his expeditions against the mountaineers he fulfilled his duty to his sovereign ; but no act of tyranny is recorded against him. It is, indeed, to be regretted, that so brave, so good a man, had not been engaged in some enterprise which, even if unsuccessful, would have shed a radiance over his fame as a military man ; for to be defeated by rude, half-armed mountaineers must indeed have been mortifying to a gallant officer conscious of his own merits. But what courage, what talents, what foresight could succeed against a people the most warlike and subtle perhaps existing, and inhabiting a country so inaccessible that its passes and fastnesses were only known to themselves !"

Having been personally known to General Willemineff, I could not, in spite of my good wishes for the Circassian cause, avoid sympathizing with his mortification at the unexpected defeat a detachment of his army experienced in the valley of Zemes, which I will attempt to describe in a future chapter.

CHAPTER XI.

Tempests in the Caucasus—Anticipated by the natives—
A Circassian Bivouac—Felt tents—Primitive method of
constructing them—Superiority of the clothing of the
mountaineers over that of the Russians for a Guerilla
campaign—Mode of provisioning a Circassian army—
Its organization—Election of military chiefs—Domestic
government—Sangiac Sheriff—Military exercises—Polish and Russian deserters—The Lesghians—Their peculiar tactics — Invasion of the Russian territory by the
mountaineers—Its consequences.

THE long-continued fine weather I had enjoyed
since my second visit to the Caucasus, so cheer-
ing to the traveller, particularly in a country
destitute of the conveniences of civilized life, was
at length succeeded by incessant rain, accompanied with gusts of wind so violent as to resemble a hurricane.   The limpid Ubin I had so much
admired as a peaceful stream gliding over its
rocky bed, was now swelled to a mighty torrent ;
while every spring and rivulet, whose tiny cur-

rents were hitherto almost invisible, roared like
so many cataracts. It was a grand, a picturesque
scene, and imparted a character so different to
the aspect of the country, that, were it not for
the presence of the hostile tribes in their peculiar
costume, I might have fancied myself overtaken
by a mountain tempest in the Tyrol.

We were, however, in some degree, prepared
for this sudden change in the weather, because,
in this land of nature, the experienced mountaineer, ignorant of the science of civilized countries to guide him in meteorological matters,
grounds his calculations on the objects of creation around him. The various tribes of insects,
from the butterfly that sports in the air to the
grasshopper that gambols in the meadows, together with the flowers that enamel the fields, are
to him the simple but unerring indications of
every variation in the atmosphere; above all, he
depends on the mists which wreath the mountain
top; and how often during our ride did my comrades intently regard the gigantic Mount Scho-
galesh, then enveloped, from its base to its summit in many-tinted vapours, which invariably
predict a change of weather. Mount Schoga-
lesh possessing, like all calcareous hills, the

property of attracting the redundant moisture
of the atmosphere, hence becomes a barometer
to the natives unerring in its accuracy : add to
which, the degree of rain and wind to be expected
is said to be calculated by the colour, denseness,
and extent of the vapour.

The different preparations made by this primitive people against the approaching storm, formed,
to a European, a novel and interesting scene; nor
were their abstemious habits, and manner of living
in the camp, less deserving attention,—proving
how little is necessary to the maintainance of an
army actuated by one common feeling of independence, and love for their fatherland.

On the first grumble of the angry elements,
the most expert seaman never exerted himself
with greater promptitude to furl his canvass than
did these athletic mountaineers to erect their
simple tents. In lieu of the poles used on these occasions, branches of trees were speedily cut down,
and bales of felt and mats unpacked wherewith to
cover them ; for no Circassian ever leaves home
without these indispensable necessaries in a
mountainous region, thinly inhabited, and where
it frequently happens that in a few minutes the
finest weather is succeeded by an overwhelming

tempest; and such was the violence with which it now raged, that even those who, either less provident, or from their hardy habits disdaining such a precaution, had omitted to furnish themselves with these temporary homes, now gladly sought shelter in the cleft of a rock, or the trunk of an aged oak; so that in a few minutes not one out of the thousands composing the camp was left without a retreat.

When we take into consideration the water-proof texture of the Circassian *tchaouka*, a capacious cloak made from a mixture of long sheep's wool and goats' hair, there is no soldier better provided, at least so far as clothing is concerned, with the means of sustaining the vicissitudes of a guerilla campaign. A Circassian, enveloped in his cloak, and sheltered beneath his felt tent, may bid defiance to the elements, while the unfortunate Russian soldier, in his flimsy jacket, linen trousers, and thread-bare surtout, and with no other retreat from the tempest than his canvas tent, and too frequently even destitute of that, is certain to be invalided after one or two summer campaigns in the Caucasus,—a result no doubt accelerated by his intemperance, particularly in vodka drinking, a vice in which they are encouraged by their own officers, for the purpose of exciting them in their attacks against the mountaineers.

The thick felt of which the Circassian tents were composed, appeared to me a substance admirably adapted for the purpose. This was the outward covering, the inside being hung with mats, most ingeniously made from sedge and a species of long grass, a manufacture equally water-proof, and one in which the Circassians are unrivalled. These poor people informed me that previous to the blockade of their coast by Russia, their manufacture of mats formed the most extensive article of export in their commerce with the Turks and Persians, owing to the circumstance of a similar species of mat being universally used for covering the floors of the mosques and public buildings, — a privation, among a hundred others, now bitterly complained of, as the Turks and Persians were accustomed to exchange for them all the little luxuries so indispensable to a people however simple in their habits ; besides, thousands were employed in manufacturing them during the winter months, who could not more advantageously occupy their time.

The simple manner iń which their tents were erected deserves attention, and might be advantageously employed by light troops while engaged in a similar species of warfare. Two poles, or rather branches of trees, are fixed in the earth, and transversely fastened at the top; to suspend the coverings over them, and tie the cords to the root of a tree, is only the work of a few minutes.

The tents of those more fastidious in their tastes were composed of several pieces of strong felt, which when connected resembled a bee-hive, and formed altogether a most convenient little dwelling, as they were generally furnished with a carpet to repose on, and a chimney to convey away the smoke; the whole, with the exception of the wood work and poles, (which can be prepared, where it is intended to bivouac for the night, in less than a quarter of an hour,) may be rolled up into a compass sufficiently small to be carried on horseback.

In justice, however, to my hardy comrades, I ought to observe that the most commodious tents were invariably appropriated to the use of the women and invalids, luxury and effeminate habits being considered in the Caucasus highly reproachful to a warrior.

Having said thus much on the Circassian manner of bivouacking, the reader will naturally inquire how such large bodies of men are to be provisioned, and what degree of discipline is preserved among them. Their very abstemious manner of living I have already noticed in my preceding volumes; bags of barley-meal, millet, Indian corn, rice, sour milk, and mead, being the principal articles of their travelling menage. Wood to make a fire is everywhere found, and stones to bake their bread upon are equally common; while hares, deer, wild boar, and, indeed, game of every description, form no bad substitute for beef and mutton,—not forgetting abundance of wild turkeys and pheasants, which are natives of the country.

Every Circassian provides himself with the above-mentioned articles previously to setting forth on his campaigning expedition; and the effect of perhaps a dozen little bags attached to the saddle, together with various other kinds of provisions, such as game, &c. picked up during their route, do not, it must be confessed, contribute to the heroic appearance of a Circassian warrior, nor do they very well correspond with the jewelled poniard and glittering armour when

K 2

it happens to be a prince. They disembarrass
themselves, however, of every encumbrance prior
to going into action.

Should this stock of provisions become exhausted, either by the length of the contest or
other causes, the warrior is supplied by the chiefs
and elders of the first tribe he meets with, the
Circassians considering the gallant soldier who
volunteers in the cause of his country entitled to
every hospitality that can be rendered to him,
even to as much as is spontaneously accorded to
the minstrel who chaunts the deeds of their heroic
ancestors, and conveys intelligence from distant
tribes.

Independent of their own stock of provisions,
and what the woods and rivers afford, the camp
is often supplied with abundance of fine cattle,
which the shepherds either present gratuitously,
or barter for some trifling article, having no better
method of disposing of them since their commerce with Turkey has been interrupted. With
respect to military pay, they have none, it being
considered the greatest disgrace in a soldier to
receive remuneration for his services to his
country. Should the hereditary prince or elder
of a tribe be found incompetent to lead his fol-

lowers to battle, a military chief is elected,—the only qualifications for this important office being, eloquence in council, heroic bravery, dexterity as a hunter, and an unerring aim as a marksman. During the time he exercises this authority, his commands are implicitly and cheerfully obeyed. Again, the military chiefs of these allied tribes elect from their own body a superior, who assumes the title of *Seraskier;* in virtue of this office he is invested with the supreme command of a certain district, and regulates every affair connected with the war. A Circassian who may have served in the armies of a neighbouring power, Turkey or Persia, is usually preferred for this office.

These Seraskiers, during the time of war, exercise almost unlimited authority. When it is possible, they meet together, and hold councils as to the best means of conducting an expedition. When circumstances forbid this, they communicate with each other by messengers; and as the office of messenger is one of high trust and confidence, none are selected but such as bear an unimpeachable character for fidelity, a character seldom or ever forfeited among these people; for even when intercepted by the enemy, and wealth and honours are weighed in the balance against a cruel death, the latter is always preferred to the ignominy of betraying his countrymen, and bringing eternal disgrace upon his name and family.

The chiefs, in conjunction with the elders of each tribe, regulate the whole of the civil and military affairs of the community over which they preside. When a man is killed in defence of the country, his family is provided for at the public cost. In the same manner, if a village or tribe suffer from the devastations of the enemy, their losses are repaired at the general expense. Or, should a tribe be driven from the lands occupied by their ancestors, through the encroachments of their powerful neighbour, Russia, they are received with open hospitality by any of the neighbouring tribes, who assign them lands, and flocks, and herds, as every addition to the numbers of a tribe adds to its power and weight in the general assembly of the nation. In such a case, the homeless refugees never fail to adopt the tribe of their benefactors, and thus become subject to the same laws, and incur the same penalties by their infraction.

The priests and elders of the tribes are the guardians of the *new Sangiac Sheriff*, which, like that of the Turks, is never to be unfurled except when the enemy's territory is about to be invaded, or in the event of the most imminent danger to the safety of the tribe, when every man capable of bearing arms is compelled to join the standard, or brand himself and family for ever with the stigma of cowardice.

As the Circassians have no regular system of discipline or tactics beyond the simple service of guerilla warfare, they amuse themselves in the camp practising all the various athletic exercises which tend to give strength and agility to the frame ; while the veterans, rendered incapable from age of taking an active part in their sports, employ themselves, among other occupations, in instructing the youths in the use of the sword, throwing the javelin, and shooting at a mark with bows and arrows ; the musket, owing to the scarcity of powder, being now never used, except when directed to the breast of the enemy.

Since the late confederation, the private feuds of the chiefs and tribes, which had hitherto depopulated the Caucasus, have nearly ceased to exist. Still, even now, a violent quarrel, or an old family feud, terminating with loss of life, is not unfrequent at their public meetings, notwithstanding the strict orders of their chiefs and elders, and the severity with which they punish the offenders.

However much the mountaineers as individuals may have suffered from the effects of the Russian invasion, on the other hand it has been productive to them of considerable advantage as a nation, and may be the means of introducing a desire to become acquainted with, and imitate the institutions of, European society. The sense of common danger has also taught them that unity and consolidation is power; while from the Polish and Russian deserters they have learned many of the arts of civilized life. These men also, by their implacable hatred to their late masters, and the fear of being taken by their former comrades, tend to inflame still more the hostility of the Circassians towards their invaders.

The well trained bands of hundreds of Lesghians, Ingushes, and other tribes, who have been lately driven from their own fastnesses in the Eastern Caucasus, a brave people, and more scientific in their system of warfare than any other of the Caucasian tribes—real veterans in their contest with Russia, whom they have obstinately and determinately resisted for upwards of

a century, will also be highly serviceable to their
new allies, by introducing order and a better
system of tactics into their armies. The weapons
of the Lesghians are the same as those of the
Circassians; and if the men are not quite so well
grown, nor possess the same physical force, they
are not less brave and intrepid in the field, and
none are superior to them as marksmen.

The peculiar tactics of the Lesghians, called, by
the Circassians, Khannoatsche, in manœuvring
their bands, appear to be already gaining ground
among some of the tribes of the Western Caucasus,
and, in the absence of a better system, will probably become generally adopted. Still, however
much the tactics of the Lesghians have been found
serviceable on the treeless mountains, and the
steppe near the Caspian Sea, the system of bush
fighting now practised by the Circassians, if a
little more order and method were introduced, is
that best adapted to the nature of the country,
the most murderous, and the most dreaded by
the Russians; for if they once descend into the
plains, and act on the offensive, their subjugation
or extermination is not far distant.

This was actually the case during the time I
was in the Caucasus. The mountaineers, ele-

vated by their temporary advantages, formed the
resolution of crossing the Kouban, for the purpose of carrying fire and sword into the land of
their enemy.   In the hope of succeeding in their
enterprise, one of their bravest Seraskiers, the
valiant Hirsis Oglou, having seized the Sangiac
Sheriff, placed himself at the head of the finest
youths of the Nottakhaitzi, Demirghoi, and other
tribes inhabiting the Kusch-haa, amounting to
about five thousand men : they did, it is true,
ravage the country of the Tchernemorsky Cossacks, and carry off several hundred head of cattle,
together with a few prisoners ; but they paid
dearly for their temerity, as they were met on
their return, between Anapa and the Kouban, by
the garrison of that town, in conjunction with a
formidable body of Cossacks.   With such a force
to contend against, had it not been for the fleetness of their horses, and their own uncommon
bravery in cutting their way through every obstacle, the mountaineers must have experienced
a most disastrous retreat ; while, in all probability, if the artillery had had time to take up a position, with their guns, according to custom, cram-
med to the muzzle with grape shot, not a single
man would have regained his home.   As it was,

it cost their heroic leader his life, and the carnage will long be remembered by many a fond mother and affectionate wife.

A Lesghian chief, according to the number of his men and the nature of the ground about to become the theatre of the contest, forms his men into bodies of from one to two hundred or more, over which he places a chief; these again he divides into platoons of ten, twenty, &c., and at the head of each appoints a soldier of experience, who, in addition to his usual weapons, carries a small lance with a flag attached to it. These flags being of different colours, each platoon in action or manœuvring recognises its own ; hence one commander is sufficient to manœuvre a large body of men, who execute every movement, at the sound of the tambourine or drum, with the greatest precision. For this purpose, the subordinate chief is usually accompanied by a drummer ; but if this useful co-adjutor cannot be found, he suspends a couple of small kettle-drums from his own girdle. The effect of a large body of men, with their many coloured flags, in motion, is at once highly picturesque and animated.

CHAPTER XII.

Alarming reports of the advance of the Russian army—
Preparation of the mountaineers to meet the enemy—
Fatal passage of the Russians through the defiles of the
Caucasus—The attack—Successful issue of the cam-
paign to the Circassians—Humane conduct of that
people towards their prisoners.

At length the storm that had raged so furiously
for more than two days without the slightest
intermission, was succeeded by a peaceful calm ;
and the sun, which had been obscured by dense
masses of angry clouds, now shone forth in all
its splendour, converting a country at all times
picturesque and lovely into a very paradise.
The feathered tribes warbled in every tree, and
innumerable insects, brilliant and gaudy, sported
from flower to flower.   In short, all created
nature seemed animated and happy.   The tents
poured forth their inhabitants ; youths and

veterans resumed their sports and duties ; whilst
the women, in their long white veils and flowing
robes, mingled cheerfully among the throng, imparting a still more picturesque effect to a scene
only to be found in the Caucasus.

There was the gallant chieftain in his glittering
chain armour, in one part of the field, coursing
on his noble steed ; in another, groups of
athletic youths, wrestling, running, or throwing
the javelin ; here, a party, with bended bow and
case full of arrows, shooting at a mark ; there,
another practising with the sword ; while, at the
same time, the surrounding hills echoed with the
shouts of the huntsmen and the cry of the dogs
in full pursuit of the game.

It seemed as if amusement were the only occupation—as if the campaign were already concluded, at least for this year. How delusive was
the calm ! In the midst of this apparent security,
all at once numerous lights gleamed through the
dense foliage on the mountain-top with a fiery
redness, (prophetic of the approaching struggle,)
which was soon followed by a crash of cannon
fearfully reverberating from valley to mountain,
from glen to hill. " *Urus ! Urus !*—the Russians !
the Russians !" burst at once from the immense

multitude; and in a few minutes several scouts, on their foaming steeds, galloped down the dizzy height. The Circassians, without waiting to hold a council of war, instantly galloped forth to the assistance of their comrades,—some to the valley of the Zemes, and others to the pass of the Bakan, where it was ascertained that the combat had commenced, leaving, however, a strong body of veterans to guard every approach to their villages, in case of surprise.

As we proceeded on our route, we found the inhabitants everywhere in motion, making the most active preparation to receive their unwelcome guests. Hundreds were on their way to enrol themselves under the command of the military chief of their tribe, and hundreds of others were engaged in making barricades across the narrow passes with huge trees and every other unwieldy material. This was done with the two-fold view of arresting the progress of the enemy and of enabling their friends to conduct the women and children, with their flocks and herds, to retreats of comparative safety; these retreats were generally the summit of some high hill or deep glen, the approaches to which were only known to themselves.

After seven or eight hours' gallop across the hills, we descended into a deep gorge, watered by the Zemes, which runs into the bay of Soudjouk-Kalé. Here we took up a position, while the main body of our party hastened to the assistance of the confederated tribes that had encamped in the defile of the Bakan leading to Anapa. This was resolved in consequence of a heavy cannonading heard in that quarter, it being presumed that the garrison of Anapa had made a sortie, and attacked the camp.

We had not been long in our new position before we were joined by parties of flying Circassians that had been completely routed by the Russians in the vicinity of Soudjouk-Kalé; they were accompanied by one or two deserters, from whom we learned that the Russian entrenchments, in consequence of the late rains, had become untenable, and that the army would most certainly attempt retreating to Ahapa that night, or the next morning.

On the receipt of this intelligence, our Seraskier conjectured the real intentions of the general in thus endeavouring to create a diversion near Anapa. He also saw the necessity of circumventing his plan, and therefore immediately dispatched from two to three hundred of his bravest, trustiest, and best-mounted horsemen, to the chiefs of the tribes encamped in the Bakan, explaining to them the ruse of the general, and counselling them, at the same time, not to be allured from their ambuscade by any sortie, but to lie in wait, and harass the enemy in their retreat, and, above all, not to hazard a general engagement.

We remained under arms the whole night, expecting the approach of the enemy, the Seraskier having judiciously posted his men among the rocks and brushwood that skirted the gorge through which it was expected the main body of the Russians would be likely to pass on their route to Anapa; and there they lay, in the same manner as a tiger crouches in his lair, watching a favourable moment to immolate his victim; and though there were upwards of five hundred men, and the greater number on horseback, not a sound was heard above a whisper,—even the horses, so admirably were they trained, remained perfectly silent.

About day-break the silence was interrupted for a few minutes by the arrival of the scouts, as they burst through the almost impenetrable thickets, with the intelligence that the enemy

were already in motion. At this instant the
scene was grand and imposing. There was the
foaming surge of the mountain stream swelled to
a torrent by the late rains,—the beetling rocks, in
all their varied and grotesque forms,—the dark
foliage of the gigantic trees,—and the summits of
the encircling hills crimsoned with the roseate
blushes of the rising sun. Nor were the athletic
forms of the highlanders, in all their varied and
picturesque attitudes, the returning scouts spur-
ring their horses up the almost perpendicular
sides of the terrific glen, less striking and novel.

Here were the well-trained bands of civilized
Europe, skilled in every art of modern warfare,
and supplied with all its *materiel*, about to be
opposed by a mountain horde of benighted Asia,
with no other fortifications than their own rocks
and brushwood—no other artillery than the rifle
and the arrow. It was, indeed, a moment of
breathless interest, and the intense solicitude de-
picted on the countenances of all shewed how
much depended on the issue of the contest.

At length the Russian columns were seen advancing, cautiously and stealthily, preceded by
their light howitzers transported on the backs of
horses, while a party of Cossacks scoured the

sides of the hills, in order to prevent the possibility of the main body of the army being taken by surprise; then, again, owing to the narrowness of the gorge and its serpentine windings, they were concealed from view, when suddenly, on doubling a curve, they came in front of their hitherto invisible enemy, who had converted every jutting crag, shrub, and tree, into an ambuscade, and were now waiting, in breathless anxiety, to deal a piece-meal destruction on the hosts of their enemy, who could not amount to less than between five and six thousand. The formidable Circassian dagger and a flight of arrows silently despatched such of the unlucky Cossacks as came within grasp of their lurking foes; and before the army were made sensible of the vicinity of so much danger, they were assailed with a shower of bullets and arrows, accompanied with one of the most terrific war whoops ever uttered by an enemy, more resembling the yell of furies than the war-cry* of mortal men, itself sufficient to

---

* I have been assured, by several Russian officers who had served in the army of the Caucasus, that this terrific cry, when heard for the first time, has frequently produced insanity in their men. It resembles, as I mentioned in my preceding work, the cry of the jackall when hunting after its prey.

infuse terror into any European, however stout-
hearted, when he heard it for the first time.

The consequences of so sudden a surprise might
have been far more fatal to the Russian troops,
but for the bravery and *sang-froid* of the officers,
who, with a great deal of trouble, succeeded in
preserving order. It may be as well to observe
that, for the sake of eluding observation, they
were on this occasion attired in the same dress
as their men.

The Russian commander, influenced, no doubt,
by prudential considerations and the impossibility
of dislodging his assailants from their fastnesses,
made no attempt to repel the aggression beyond
a few volleys from his light artillery, which had
no other effect than that of keeping the great
body of the mountaineers at a respectful distance.
Even in defiance of these, a few daring spirits,
notwithstanding the positive commands of their
chiefs, not only grappled here and there for a
moment with the panic-struck troops, when a
favourable opportunity presented itself, but continued to hover about and harass them in their
march, until they arrived within a few miles of
Anapa, where a dreadful conflict took place between them and the united bands of the Nottak-

haitzi, the Demirghoi, and the Khapsoukhie; and had it not been for the succour of the garrison of that fortress, and the arrival of a strong body of Tchernemorsky Cossacks, to which we may add, the want of ammunition and a proper combination on the part of the Circassians, the carnage would undoubtedly have been dreadful; as it was, their losses were immense, for, if the accounts of the deserters might be relied upon, out of the immense force with which General Willemineff commenced the campaign in May, only a few thousands escaped the devouring sword of the mountaineers, and the not less fatal fevers that raged in his camp.

CHAPTER XIII.

Return to Soudjouk-Kalé—Defeat of the tribes in its vicinity by the Russians — The Caucasian guerilla — His
revengeful disposition—Causes of this—Generosity natural to the character of a Circassian knight—Predatory
disposition of the Caucasians—Cossacks and Tartars—
Their desertion to the Circassians—Visit of the Emperor
to the Caucasus—Effects of the war to Russia—Success
of the mountaineers in their predatory expeditions.

WITH a view to relieve the adjoining villages,
and to assist in expelling whatever force the
Russian general might have left in his temporary
camp in the bay of Soudjouk-Kalé, our Seraskier
continued his march towards the sea-coast. It
was, however, unnecessary, as the campaign was
completely at an end for the present year, the
Russians having entirely abandoned their positions in the bay, a circumstance which we learned
from the straggling bands of Achmet Ali, Beislam-
bey and Hadgi-bey, chiefs of the tribes inhabiting
the neighbourhood of Soudjouk-Kalé, and those of

Upper Abasia, the whole of whom had suffered considerably during their late encounter with the Russians in the valley of Soudjouk.

According to their accounts it appeared that one of their own chiefs, at the head of several hundred of his clansmen, were in close pursuit of another detachment of the enemy that had taken a more difficult passage across the mountains to Anapa.

This we subsequently ascertained to have been a ruse of the general, who, after a sharp engagement with the mountaineers, succeeded in dispersing them, and in order to divert their attention from his real object, had sent the detachment alluded to, hoping, by means of this stratagem, to secure a safe passage through the valley of the Zemes for his artillery and the great bulk of his army, with the wounded and invalids. His scheme was, however, in some degree frustrated, for he was unexpectedly met by our Seraskier, who, if he had only retained the chosen body of men he despatched to the assistance of his allies encamped in the defile of the Bakan, would assuredly have been able, from the admirable position he had taken, to annoy the Russian troops in no inconsiderable degree.

On approaching the coast, we witnessed, in

every direction, the devastating effects of the
summer's campaign in the ruined villages of the
mountaineers, and the still unburied bodies of
the Russian soldiers. Piles of huge trees lay
about the valley, having been cut down by the
invaders for the purpose of forming a passage to
transport their artillery, and which the natives
had availed themselves of to serve as temporary
fortifications in their deadly struggle to repel the
advance of the enemy into the interior. The
whole prospect was indeed deplorable, being the
picture of a land that had just suffered all the
horrors of a general conflagration.

When we consider the excited state of a people
in the situation of the Caucasians, engaged in a
struggle for home, for freedom, for life, actuated
universally by a hatred the most implacable towards the whole Russian nation, we cannot be
surprised to learn that the greater number of the
wounded and straggling soldiers belonging to the
Russian camp fell victims to the swords of their
unrelenting enemy.

This intense hatred against the Russians arises
not so much from any peculiarly sanguinary disposition as from a desire to act in accordance
with the precepts of their religion, to obey the

dying injunctions of their fathers, and the commands of their elders. Their wives, their friends, in short, all those they hold dear on earth,—or, when dead, whose memory they revere,—impose upon them the destruction of a nation whose sword has been crimsoned a thousand times in the best blood of their ancestors.

Revenge! revenge! is with them paramount to every other consideration ; no wealth can purchase forbearance, no entreaty for mercy can avert the blow ; blood must be requited alone by blood ; for when a Caucasian falls, hundreds of his comrades vow to avenge his death,—and until that vow is accomplished, their hearts are steeled to every pleading of pity or humanity.

This revengeful disposition is fostered not only by the encouragement it receives from their religious tenets, but by the opinion they entertain that every Russian they slay appeases by his death the unquiet spirit of some lamented warrior who fell on the field of battle, and never could rest in peace till his blood was avenged.

Hence a Caucasian regards the immolation of an enemy as a deed which calls upon him to rejoice, as the fulfilment of a solemn promise given at the death of a comrade in arms, as a debt of

gratitude paid to the manes of those brave warriors who fought and bled for their country.

With such feelings, and actuated by such motives, the unlucky Russian soldier that happens
to fall within the murderous grasp of so formidable an enemy as the guerilla of the Caucasus has
little chance of escape, unless through the inter-
ference of some chief, who, prompted by humanity
or avarice, stays the hand of his clansman, and
reserves to himself the disposal of the prisoner.
Numbers, however, continue to escape on declaring themselves to be Tartars or Poles, whom
the Caucasians regard as fellow-sufferers, and as
serving in the Russian ranks by compulsion : but
if on this plea their lives are spared, death is only
commuted for slavery, no confidence being now
placed by the mountaineers in the assertion of
any Russian soldier with respect to his country,
unless some Caucasian or refugee happens to be
able to establish the truth of his declaration.

This caution has been rendered indispensible
by the repeated instances in which the Russian
spies have found means in this manner to elude
their vigilance.

The strictness of the Russian blockade has also
tended to render the Caucasians even more than

usually relentless towards their prisoners, as they are now deprived of the channel by which they formerly disposed of such as fell into their hands as slaves to the Turks or Persians; whereas at present, no other resource remaining than to make them agricultural labourers, it is highly probable that many whom they cannot profitably employ are sacrificed.

Notwithstanding this inexorable spirit of revenge, imbibed by a Caucasian from his earliest infancy,—notwithstanding it is interwoven with his religion, customs, and laws,—we may often see the chivalrous Circassian knight and his clansmen rescuing a prostrate foe from the murderous grasp of some inhuman savage—an act which we cannot but admire, when we remember that they are actuated solely by a compassionate feeling, by the dictates of a generous disposition.

The example of the Circassians in this respect, although that of a people so low in the scale of knowledge and civilization, might be followed with advantage by some of the European nations who pride themselves in the proficiency they have attained in the one, in the progress they have made in the other, and who, though professing a religion which breathes only forgiveness of injuries, which inculcates every moral precept capable of ennobling human nature, yet, in the nineteenth century, commit acts of ferocious barbarity that would have disgraced savages.

However merciless may be the conduct of the majority of the Caucasians of every tribe towards their enemies in the field, they exhibit in their transactions with each other, as well as in their intercourse with the subjects of any friendly power, as much humanity, courtesy, and kindly feeling, as the most civilized among the nations of Europe. A stranger, well recommended to any one of the chiefs, may travel over the whole of the Caucasus without the slightest danger or insult.

Indeed, my remarks with reference to the revengeful disposition of the guerilla of the Caucasus do not apply, in their full extent, to the Attéghéi (Circassian) tribes, who are among the most civilized, but to their allies, the Tartars, the Lesghi, the Ingushes, the Ossetinians, and other tribes in the remote mountain districts in the vicinity of the Wladi-Kaukas, and those situated on the Caspian sea,—tribes who have been for upwards of a century at war with Russia, and have suffered deeply from her oppression. It must also, in justice to

the Russians, be observed, that they have, by
their humanity and moderation towards the inhabitants of the Western Caucasus—if we except
their unjust invasion of the country—at least di-
vested their aggression of any character of wanton
cruelty; for, since the tyrant Yermeloff ceased to
wield the baton of command, few are the acts of
tyranny recorded against the governors or their
generals in the Caucasus. Still, misery, rapine,
and destitution, are the inseparable attendants
upon war, even though carried on with every
anxiety to lessen its horrors.

Like the inhabitants of every other country,
those of the Western Caucasus are divided in
opinion respecting peace and war. A few of the
tribes residing on the coast naturally feel anxious
to see the termination of hostilities, and would
even purchase peace at the expense of becoming
vassals of the Autocrat, but in this they are over-
ruled by those residing in the interior, the most
powerful and influential, and who find it their interest to prolong a contest which tends so materially to enrich them. Besides, it affords them
an opportunity of exercising their favourite occupations—war and predatory incursions; for, secure in their own mountain fastnesses, they can

defy any enemy, however powerful, to subdue
them.

On the other hand, those who inhabit the sea-
coast, momentarily looking forward to a repetition of hostilities, their existence is marked by
incessant anxiety and watchfulness. Still, notwithstanding the long duration of the war, and
the yearly invasion of their territory, the population, according to their own accounts, is on the
increase since the treaty of Adrianople and the
suspension of their intercourse with the Turks,
who were too frequently instrumental in introducing the plague, and thereby causing even a
greater mortality than the sword of the Russians.

It must also be observed, that the mountaineers
rarely attack the enemy, unless certain of success, and then the attack is made with such boldness and rapidity, that whole ranks are mowed
down before the soldiers have time to recover
from the shock of the onset, these wily guerillas
escaping to the thickets with scarcely the loss of
a single man. Indeed, a charge of Circassians,
mounted on their fleet, well-trained steeds, and
expert as they are in the use of the sword and
the rifle, is so formidable from its impetuosity,
that no cavalry or infantry Russia has yet been

able to bring against them can withstand it. For,
unlike Europeans, they never fight in a line, but
in bodies of about twenty or thirty at a time,—
their common practice being to fall unawares
upon the enemy, and harass them day and night
during their march. After making a charge, they
disperse, then rally and return again to the charge,
when their exhausted foe supposes them to have
fled; and as they are certain to kill immediately,
or wound mortally, those whom they hit, and
never fail to avail themselves of a good position,
these circumstances, combined with their desperate bravery and perseverance, render them, perhaps, the most formidable antagonists to be found
in any country.

Although the system of fighting we have described is that usually adopted by the Circassians,
they frequently pursue a different plan, much de-
pending upon the nature of the country, the force
they may be able to collect, and the impression
they may have made in the ranks of the enemy,
who, consequently, can never depend upon their
movements. But of every other species of warfare, they most excel in pursuit; for should an
enemy, during their retreat, become in the least
disordered, a strong detachment of these well-

mounted guerillas is sufficient to destroy a whole army in detail.

One of the regulations of the confederated tribes of the Western Caucasus obliges every chief who joins it to bring with him to the camp of his district at least five hundred men, well armed, when he and his clansmen become entitled to a share in whatever plunder may be obtained in their expeditions against the Russians. Such is the cupidity of the Caucasians, so eager their desire to obtain a share in the spoil, to which we may add, their passionate attachment to war, that it has had the effect of stimulating to action whole tribes, not only in the remote districts of the Western Caucasus, but in the eastern division, which had hitherto remained tolerably peaceable.

Even the neighbouring Cossacks and Tartars have commenced deserting in great numbers to the Circassians,—that people, like wise politicians, ensuring liberty, lands, and equal rights, to every Cossack, Tartar, and Turk who joins their standard and swears to conform to their laws and customs.

It was principally these desertions, and the

late reverses of the Russian troops in the Caucasus, that induced the Emperor Nicholas to visit this part of his extensive dominions; but every exertion of the Russian government to retain the turbulent Cossacks and Tartars as faithful subjects will avail nothing, so long as Circassia remains independent, and its chiefs continue faithfully to fulfil their promises,—these warlike hordes preferring the roving, predatory life of a Caucasian guerilla to the regular service, the restraints imposed, and the slavish obedience exacted, by Russian military discipline.

The success of the mountaineers in their marauding expeditions must have been very great, since nearly every Caucasian, from the prince to the peasant, is possessed of some valuable trophy of his success against the Russians. Articles of dress, fire-arms, gold watches, platina snuff-boxes, constitute the usual spoil, taken from the soldier and the travelling merchant; while the great military and commercial road, the Wladi-Kaukas, being the medium for transporting the Russian manufactures to Georgia, &c., bales of fine cloth, silks, muslins, and cottons, frequently become the rich prizes of the roving guerilla bands infesting that part of the Caucasus, and from which, in a great measure, the splendid wardrobes of the women are supplied.

In fact, Russia has been hitherto in every respect a loser by her Caucasian contest, for, independent of the expense she has incurred year after year, her losses in men are incalculable. Dearly, indeed, has she purchased possession of the few miserable forts she holds on the sea-coast; neither must we forget the injury her reputation has sustained from the various disastrous reverses her arms have experienced in her campaigns with the mountaineers, — reverses which may at some future period have the effect of arousing the Turks and Persians to resistance, by teaching them that their dreaded foe is not invincible.

CHAPTER XIV.

Soudjouk-Kalé — Its localities—Description of the ruined
  fortress in the bay—Unfounded statements of Russia
  with respect to Soudjouk-Kalé—Excursions in the valley
  of Soudjouk-Kalé—Deplorable effects of the war—Termination of the campaign of 1836.

In relating the details of my coasting voyage
round the Black Sea, I endeavoured in some degree to familiarize my readers with the situation
of Soudjouk-Kalé; but as recent events have invested that bay with more than common interest,
perhaps a few additional particulars respecting
its localities and history may not at the present
moment be unworthy of attention. I have already
stated that it lies thirty miles south-east of Anapa;
having, however, on my second visit an opportunity of surveying the adjoining country with
more accuracy, I found the distance by land does
not exceed twenty-five miles, as we then avoid

the extensive curve necessarily made while coasting. This splendid bay—nearly eight miles in circumference — from its great depth of water, excellent anchorage, and security from violent winds, is admirably adapted either for a commercial station or a naval port. It is completely landlocked, except at one point, from about S.E. to S. by E., which might, if deemed advisable, be easily rendered secure by a mole.

To the east of the bay, a range of bleak hills, furrowed by innumerable water-courses, gradually descends from a height of about a thousand feet down to a long line of rocky shore. To the west, the hills are of somewhat less elevation, and in great part covered with wood. These also gradually diminish as they extend into the sea. So completely is this fine harbour protected on every side, that, when viewed in a north-westerly direction, it has more the appearance of a lake than a bay.

The Circassians, in their own dialect, give it the name of Tschugo-Zuck-Kaleh, or the Castle of Mice, from the circumstance of immense quantities of field-mice infesting the land in its immediate vicinity.

The fortress of Soudjouk-Kalé was undoubt-

edly of great antiquity, having been mentioned
in the earliest records of the Genoese and Vene-
tian navigators, under the name of Porto Suaco
and Porto Zurzuchi; and some writers even pretend that it was the Sindika of the ancients. The
fort, situated to the west of the bay, not far from
the sea, and formerly occupied by the Turks,
is now merely a shapeless mass of ruins. To judge
from the peculiar manufacture of some of the
bricks, and more particularly from the admirable
nature of the cement, the original edifice must
have been erected at some very distant period.
That the Turks in modern days have added to
the building is most evident, from the number of
glazed bricks we find, blue, green, and white, and
also from part of the cement being a species of
mineral clay found in the neighbourhood, and
differing entirely from the other. After having
closely examined the remains of the original
foundation, I should be inclined to conclude that
it was a regular fortified castle, rather of European
than Asiatic construction, and probably the work
of the Genoese in their best days.

The natives of the neighbouring hills now avail
themselves of the bricks in making beds for their
canals, which they very ingeniously conduct from

river to rivulet, and form reservoirs, by which
means they insure a supply of water for their
cattle during the great drought of summer.
These ruins are now somewhat dangerous to the
exploring antiquary, on account of the number of
serpents and myriads of tarantulas and other
noxious reptiles who have here taken up their
abode.

Every unprejudiced man, be his politics what
they may, who peruses my statements respecting
Soudjouk-Kalé,—the account of my visit while
coasting round the Black Sea,—the subsequent
evacuation of the bay by the Russian army,—the
verification of the fact of the fort having been
formerly a Turkish commercial station, and after-
wards laid in ruins by the Circassians,—must feel
surprised at the effrontery of Russia in claiming
it as her own, and above all, at her asserting, in
the face of the most demonstrative evidence to
the contrary, that she still possesses that fort,
and continues to garrison it with her troops.

What is still worse, this falsehood was made
the ground of an official declaration from Count
Nesselrode to his excellency the Earl of Durham,
and, unfortunately, it was received by his lordship
with unquestioning reliance upon the veracity of

his diplomatic opponent; and upon that wilful misrepresentation—a misrepresentation rare even in the annals of state intrigue—has been founded the decision come to by her Majesty's ministers relative to the capture of the Vixen, and the honour of England sacrificed.

That his excellency, whose honest intentions have never been impugned, has been the dupe of Russian artifice, cannot be doubted. But what must we think of the Russian government, and what caution should it teach England in her diplomatic intercourse with that power, who, to gain a political object, scruples not to employ fraud to secure it. When a man in private life employs false pretences to acquire money, we call it swindling; but when a government, in its public acts, is not ashamed to use the same means to obtain a valuable province, the courteous world terms it political finesse! How indulgent!

Russia probably calculated that the mist she had flung over Circassia would effectually screen her from the rude, unwished-for gaze of European curiosity, and confidently assumed, that any representation she made, however at variance with truth, would be unhesitatingly received respecting a country of which nothing except the most im-

perfect details was known. But I repeat, she has
attempted to mislead Europe and deceive England; and I defy the court of St. Petersburg,
or any one of its hireling writers in this or any
other country, to contradict the simple statements
I have brought forward, not from any enmity I
bear the Russian government, however I may despise some of its acts,—not from any wish to
embarrass that of my own country, however I
may regret the line of policy it has adopted,—
but with the view to forward the cause of a noble
people—a people, whose hospitality I experienced,
whose patriotism and virtues I admired. Above
all, I have deeply felt for the injury done to the
honour of my country, and have seen, with vexation, the extension of her commerce in this quarter of the globe, so happily commenced through
the indefatigable enterprise of her citizens, frustrated.

On leaving the ruins of Soudjouk-Kalé's once
proud castle, I rode round the extensive bay and
adjoining valley, and a more deplorable scene
than was then offered to view cannot be imagined :
there was not a single village in its vicinity, for
miles, that was not one mass of blackened ruins ;
and such had been the devastation committed

by the Russian soldiery, that we could not procure bread for ourselves, nor forage for our horses,
beyond the scanty after-grass that the mountain-
top afforded.   There was scarcely a family that
did not mourn the loss of some dear friend or
relative ; and so unequal had been the contest—
so universal the feeling that death was preferable
to slavery, that numbers even of the women
were induced to join the ranks, and fell valiantly
fighting by the side of their fathers, brothers, and
lovers.

How mournfully changed was the scene from
the aspect it presented when I was last at Soudjouk !   It is true, the lovely bay, bright and tranquil, was still there ; but the brilliant camp, the
gay throng of gallant youths, among whom I had
only a few short months previously mingled, the
sounds of revelry and mirth, all had vanished.
How many of these brave spirits had met an untimely fate in that short space of time is only
known to Russia, for her gazette records not her
hecatombs of victims in the Caucasus.

Thus ended the campaign of 1836, which had
no other effect than to exasperate still more the
Circassians against their unprincipled invaders,
waste the lives of the unfortunate Russian sol-

diers, and drain an exchequer not easily replenished in a country like Russia.

Poor General Willemineff! He had to contend, not only against the desperate bravery of the mountaineers, but with the elements; since, having completely routed the natives in the vicinity of Soudjouk-Kalé, and hoping, consequently, to establish his winter quarters on the bay, he found his plans frustrated by circumstances over which he had no control. The autumnal rains had commenced unusually early, accompanied with such violent wind as to scatter the fleet under Admiral Pallinotti, who was obliged to return to his winter anchorage at Sevastopol; hence the general was deprived of the support of a marine force. To add to his disasters, the Zemes, a mere rivulet in summer, became so swollen as to swamp his intrenchments. This, united to the scarcity of provisions and a pestilential fever that mowed down his ranks, determined him, malgré his inclinations, to evacuate his quarters, and fight his way to Anapa, having no other alternative but to do this, or allow his men to perish with hunger and disease, to say nothing of the impossibility of troops remaining in their temporary encampment, exposed to the rigour of a Cau-

casian winter; for so incessant was the hostility
of the mountaineers, that his men were unable to
erect the necessary log-houses.

Perhaps at no former period during the war
had the arms of the mountaineers been attended
with so many brilliant successes as this year, not
only in the western, but in the eastern division
of the Caucasus, the Russian army there, (styled
the Georgian,) under General Rosen, being equally
unsuccessful.

COSSACKS IN THE CAUCASUS.

CHAPTER XV.

Inal Aslan Gherrai, the Circassian chief—His character—
Inviolable faith of a Circassian chief towards his guest—
Regulations for ensuring his safety—Journey to Pchad—
Aspect of the country—Ghelendjik—Cossacks—Arrival
at the house of the chief of Pchad—Triumphant reception—The banquet—Enthusiasm of the people—The patriarchal chief of Pchad—His reverse of fortune—Exile.

I now began to think seriously of returning
homeward; for however delightful excursions may
be in a mountainous country in the summer and

autumn, a winter's residence could not be agreeable under any circumstances in the Caucasus. At the same time, I must ever feel grateful for the hospitality and kind reception I everywhere experienced among the brave mountaineers, but more particularly from the noble chieftain under whose protection I was placed,—a man from whom I received every kindness that could be heaped upon a stranger. Devotedly attached to the cause of his country, Inal Aslan-Gherrai, surnamed Bahatyre, from his uncommon strength and stature, if he does not possess the military talents necessary for a great leader, is in every way qualified for the arduous task of guerilla chief: robust in his constitution, temperate in his habits, subsisting solely upon bread and sour milk, brave and enterprising to a fault, austerely moral in his manners and conduct, he is looked up to as a saint by his followers, and implicitly obeyed by all, be his commands what they may.

This brave man descended from Arslanbeck, at one time the terror of the Russians, and by the female side* from Devlet-Gherrai, the pretender

* During the reign and after the deposition of the imbecile Sahin Gherrai, the last Khan of Krim-Tartary, whom Catharine placed on the throne in opposition to the wishes

to the throne of Krim-Tartary. His influence is very extensive among the Circassians of every tribe, and also among the Tartars established in the Western Caucasus. If he is so fortunate as to escape the Russian bullets, he will, or I am much mistaken, prove one of the most dangerous enemies that government has to dread in the Caucasus. Although he had attained high rank in the Turkish army, and basked in the sunshine of courtly favour, he now contents himself with the same fare as the meanest clansman of

of the Tartars, and subsequently deposed, usurping the sovereignty herself, Devlet Gherrai, the rival and legitimate Khan, made several ineffectual attempts to dispossess the Russians of their prize. Ardent and enterprising in his character, beloved by his countrymen, and supported by the Ottoman Porte, against a less powerful foe he might have made a successful stand; but the superior force of Russia prevailed. Defeated in almost every engagement, and his followers dispersed, he retreated to the mountains on the south coast of the Crimea, where he wandered as a fugitive, like Charles the Pretender in Scotland; and although the Russian government offered a large reward for the unfortunate prince, to the honour of the Tartars, they, like the gallant Scots, continued to protect and support their ill-fated monarch till he escaped to the Caucasus, where he soon collected a band of followers, who, under such a leader, long continued to carry fire and sword into the territory of his implacable enemy.

his tribe ; and, among his other voluntary privations, generally substitutes his tchaouka for a
mattress and covering, and his saddle for a pillow, instead of the luxuriant cushions of the
divan—self-denial being a virtue held in high
estimation in the Caucasus. Since his return to
Circassia, he has contributed not a little in animating the mountaineers in their hostility, and in
guiding their efforts by his counsels.

His animosity against Russia is doubly increased from the circumstance of his being reduced to a state of exile. Kabardia, his native
country, over a part of which his ancestors exercised the rights of chieftain from time immemorial, having become subject to Russia, his lands
were seized, his tribe either dispersed or compelled
to acknowledge the sovereignty of the conqueror,
while himself and family wandered as fugitives
either in Turkey or Persia.

When the war in the Caucasus assumed a more
important complexion, he escaped from Turkey,
accompanied by several other sultans, descendants
of Tartar chiefs, whose tribes have been scattered
or reduced to subjection by the unceasing efforts of
Russia to extend her frontier, Circassia being the
home of every refuge from Russian despotism,

whether Cossack, Pole, Turk, or Tartar, its inaccessible defiles offering a secure retreat, and its valiant inhabitants the means of retaliating upon the enemy of their country.

The Tartar princes in the Caucasus are usually distinguished by the title of Sulthaun; but our Kabardian, from being himself a Circassian, was soon elected by a tribe inhabiting the country watered by the Antihir, in the province of Khapsoukhie, as their military leader, and by the confederated chiefs as one of their Seraskiers, whose office I have already described.

The duties of hospitality every Circassian is bound to observe with the most scrupulous attention towards his brethren of the confederation; but the duties of a chief towards the stranger who places himself under his protection are still more imperative, and must be rigidly observed, according to received usage, even at the hazard of life itself; and the chief who assumes this trust is not only bound himself to defend his guest, but the whole tribe must be answerable for his preservation. Hence, a stranger in Circassia, secured with such protection, becomes an object of high interest and importance to the whole tribe, for, in the event of being murdered, or even of receiving the slightest injury, the wrong would be avenged while a single man among them was capable of bearing arms.

Moreover, in compliance with established rule among these people, the duties of a protector chief are not limited to ensuring the safety of the stranger while he remains among his own tribe, since he is equally bound to provide against danger during his continuance in the country. For this purpose he is never suffered to depart till a sufficient escort is procured; these are obliged to deliver him uninjured to the next confederate, who becomes, in like manner, answerable for his security; and thus a stranger is passed from one tribe to another, till he crosses the frontier, each escort being obliged to render to their chiefs and elders a strict account of the trust reposed in them.

On my departure, owing to the unsettled state of the country, and more especially as my route to Pchad lay in the neighbourhood of the Russian forts, Ghelendjik and Aboon, my Konak, with several hundreds of his followers, accompanied me to the residence of Mahmood Indar, chief of the small tribe I already alluded to on my arrival in the Caucasus, residing near the bay

of Pchad. We had also among our escort several of the relatives and followers of the prince of
Pchad, and, being well armed and mounted, there
was nothing to fear from the hostility of the
Russian garrisons; besides, they never attempt
to leave their fastnesses except the severest
privation compels them to sally forth in quest of
provisions.

Our route to Pchad—one day's journey on
horseback—with very little variation, was the
same as that I have already described in my preceding work, between that bay and the valley of
the Zemes, or Thumusse of the Tartars. It was
also unenlivened by adventures; a comparative
calm had succeeded the tumultuous excitement
of war,—the mountaineers had returned to their
villages from the summer's campaign, and their
flocks and herds, which had been driven to the
mountain-top for safety, were again grazing on the
sloping hills in uninterrupted tranquillity. The
women had also resumed their various avocations
in the fields, surrounded by their playful children;
in short, everything wore the aspect of returning
peace, at least for a season, and formed altogether
a beautiful picture, exhibiting every feature that
could lend a charm to pastoral life.

Instead of travelling in a northern direction, towards the fort of Aboon, as we had done in my previous excursion, we kept nearer to the sea coast, where, from the adjoining hills, we had a complete view of the sea and the fort of Ghelendjik, then surrounded by its little encampment of Cossacks, who, in their temporary guardhouses, made from branches of trees and sedges, were enjoying at the same time the autumnal sun and their beloved vodka.

Several of our wild youths, more with the intention of amusing themselves at the expense of the Russian soldiers than of injuring them, and, no doubt, desirous of shewing the proficiency they had acquired in bush-fighting to their graver comrades, stole unperceived, like serpents creeping through the grass, on the sentinels, and discharged among them a volley of arrows, which caused the groups of bacchanalians to retreat most precipitately.   If it were not that one or two of the poor fellows were stretched lifeless, we might have found food enough for merriment, as vodka and bottles were scattered in a moment; while the drinkers themselves, without even waiting to seize their weapons, rushed helter-skelter into the fort, as if they momentarily expected to be overwhelmed by an avalanche. This unceremonious salute was returned by one from the garrison, which had no other effect than that of interrupting the stillness of the forest by its loud reverberations; indeed, they might as well have sent their grape shot into the depths of the sea: our position on the heights placing us completely out of danger, and as for the young perpetrators, being mounted on their fleet steeds, they were almost instantly lost in the recesses of the forest.

As we passed onward in our route, every village and hamlet was the scene of a triumph to my brave companions; they were blessed by the aged, caressed by the young, and feasted wherever they halted. But it was on approaching the pretty little cot, or rather cluster of cots, belonging to the prince of Pchad, that a scene was presented highly characteristic of the simple, patriarchal habits of the Circassians, and which will never be effaced from my memory.

It appears that a custom prevails in this part of the Western Caucasus, when a campaign is terminated, for the different clans to greet their respective chiefs with a triumph on their return home,

and I now witnessed that given to welcome the sons
of the patriarch of Pchad. When the train of warriors entered the little territory of the prince, they
were met by numbers of young women from the
neighbouring villages and hamlets, who strewed
their path with branches of trees and flowers, while
the old men and women, in groups, implored,
with uplifted arms, the blessings of Heaven on
the brave defenders of their country's independence; at the same time the song of the bard
and the strain of the minstrel were raised to
celebrate their deeds and imprecate curses upon
their unprincipled invaders, whom they branded
with a variety of epithets, which I trust, for the
honour of the Russian soldier, were more poetical
than true.   Among others, they were denounced
as skulking cowards, who never shew fight except when protected by intrenchments or cannon.
Their affectionate reception by their wives and
families repaid the hardy warriors for the privations they had endured, for the perils they had
encountered; and the conviction that at least a
temporary respite from the toils of war had been
won, gave a character of security to their re-
joicings.

It was, however, Mahmood, the old prince himself, that riveted my attention. He was, as my companions assured me, nearly a hundred years of age; and I much regret that it is impossible to convey, by description, any correct idea of the appearance of the gallant old warrior. Although age had furrowed his expressive countenance with deep lines, and blanched his flowing beard, his eye still glowed with the fire of youth. Although his attenuated figure bore the stamp of frail mortality, he stood erect and firm, and was as completely armed as the youngest warrior of his tribe; and, as may be supposed, in a land where age is more respected than in the most civilized country in Europe, the influence of the patriarch of Pchad was powerful and extensive, both among his own tribe and also with the neighbouring chiefs.

We met at the house of Mahmood several chiefs from Upper Abasia, and bountifully, indeed, did the good old man spread the board of hospitality; his sheep were slaughtered wholesale, the poultry-yard was deprived of its inhabitants, while the produce of the dairy and the bees was lavishly expended in preparing every little luxury which the culinary skill of his family could invent. In addition to these, hundreds of skins were emptied of a very agreeably-flavoured wine, for on this occasion even the most rigid relinquished their austere habits, and abandoned themselves to mirth and enjoyment.   It was the triumph of a people to celebrate the success of their arms, to reconcile the feuds of chief and chief, to cement the union of tribe and tribe.   The song of the minstrel spoke of gladness and hope; and the hardy warriors, over whom time had shed wisdom, exhorted their followers, in animated orations, to preserve unanimity in their councils, to act with courage in the field, and to hurl destruction on their invaders, which never failed to be responded to by the tumultuous shouts of the auditory and the clash of hundreds of swords.

It would, perhaps, be but time wasted to expatiate on the enthusiasm of this interesting people, on their resignation and cheerfulness in the midst of so many privations and dangers, as my representations might be deemed by some too highly coloured, and by others as emanating from a too partial predilection for the cause of Circassian independence.   Let, however, the conclusions of those who may have no sympathy beyond their own contracted circle be what they may, I saw enough

during my short visit to the Caucasus to influence
me powerfully in favour of that brave people,
and, being regarded by all merely as a Stambouli-
hakkim, there was no effort made to bias my
judgment. Indeed, were it not for the dear friends
who tremblingly awaited my return, my humble
efforts should have been devoted to their cause,
so long as a hostile soldier of Russia desecrated
their soil.

I have never allowed my political bias (for a
traveller should have none) to influence my representations either of countries or their inhabitants : I may, however, say thus much, that I am
neither friendly to rebellion nor to republicanism,
for long experience and an intimate acquaintance
with every form of government, has taught me
that a controlled monarchy, such as we happily
possess in England, is that which tends most to
the happiness of the people, to the establishment
of social order, the preservation of morality, in
short, to insure the blessings of civilized life.
Not one line, therefore, of these pages would
have been dedicated to the cause of the Circassians in their struggle with Russia, however much
I might abhor despotism, if I entertained the

opinion that they were her subjects in arms against her legitimate authority.

The present patriarchal form of government in Circassia is admirably adapted to the necessities of a people simple in their habits ; but when steam navigation and commerce shall have introduced among them the knowledge of the wants, and, I must add, the vices, of civilization, it is but too probable, if they do not fall beneath the sway of despotic Russia, the country will become a prey to intestine feuds, similar to those which so long distracted, then ruined, and finally enslaved, Poland,—unless some great influential chief shall proclaim himself sovereign, and establish a monarchy ; an event by no means improbable.

If any benefits could result to the natives of the Western Caucasus, from their subjugation to Russia, any amelioration in their social condition, similar to that which has resulted from the British sway in India, we might, in some degree, be reconciled to their fate. The conquests of England in India have been indeed a blessing to the benighted inhabitants; her mild rule, just laws, and civilized institutions, have spread a halo of brightness over the hundred millions that acknowledge her supremacy in that vast region,—a consummation effected more by the hand of Providence for its own good purposes, rather than by the agency of political wisdom, or the force of arms.

Not so with Russia; her rapacious legions, led on for the most part by penniless, unprincipled adventurers, march forth to conquest with the hope of plunder for a guiding star, and enforce at the point of the bayonet a form of religion, debased by superstitious and unmeaning ceremonies, tending more to the encouragement of vice and immorality than the propagation of the humanizing truths of our divine instructor. Assuredly, the day of retribution cannot be far distant; if Europe tacitly sanctions an act of such flagrant injustice as the conquest of the Caucasus, One All-Powerful will at length crush those who have consummated the downfall and misery of its unhappy inhabitants.

But, to return to the patriarchal chieftain.* Poor old Mahmood! how much I admired thy

* The summer subsequent to my visit to Circassia, Pchad was taken by the Russians, who have commenced building a fort; and the port dues, which formed the principal revenue of the fugitive prince, now increase the exchequer of the Autocrat of the North.

peaceful retreat,—the beautiful rivulet that bab-
bled past thy door, the gigantic linden thou hadst
planted with thine own hands, the sunny slopes
of the majestic hills, covered with thy flocks and
herds, the manly youths of thy lineage, the beautiful daughters of thy house, and the little rosy
cherubs that called thee great-grandfather! But,
alas! in this world of care, with an ambitious
neighbour, like a ravenous wolf prowling about
a pen-fold, little didst either thou or thy gallant
tribe expect that one short winter would leave
thee without a home,—a refugee, a wanderer, in
the fastnesses of thy native hills.

No longer will thy humble cots be open for the
reception of the wearied traveller—no longer will
thy osier palace echo to the song of revelry, the
feast of triumph: the knout and the lash will
succeed thy patriarchal reproof; and in a little
time thy brave tribe, now become the slaves of a
despot, will degenerate from the bravest of the
brave to the veriest cowards,—mere hewers of
wood and drawers of water to their conquerors.

Unhappy Mahmood! hard indeed has been thy
fate: after passing a hundred winters as the son of
a chief and the chieftain of thy tribe, how melancholy is it that destiny has decreed thou shouldst

not pass the brief space thou canst hope to sojourn in this world of sorrow in the land, the house, of thy ancestors,—the patriarch, the sage, of thy tribe. How much happier would have been thy last moments if thou hadst breathed them, as thou hadst lived, an independent chief! But no, poor old man! if thou hast survived thy misfortunes, another home must be thy resting-place, —thy grave must be dug in a strange land!

CHAPTER XVI.

The province of Khapsoukhie—Its localities—Productions
—Singular intoxicating honey of the Caucasus—Stone
honey—Wines—Rivers—Occupation of the natives—
Singular waggons—Industry of the women—Cattle—
Inconveniences resulting to the Circassians from the
blockade of their coast by Russia.

As I am now about to leave the province of
Khapsoukhie, perhaps a few additional particulars
relative to its localities &c. may not be altogether
uninteresting. The whole of the extensive country
bordering the Euxine, from the little territory of
the prince of Pchad, to Anapa, is inhabited by the
Khapsoukhie tribes, the most powerful and the
most numerous of all the Circassians in the
Western Caucasus. This highly-favoured district
cannot be surpassed in picturesque beauty by any
other country that, like it, does not number
among its features the towering castle, the expansive lake, and the sublime alp. The majestic

hills are, for the most part, covered with splendid trees,—the oak, beech, linden, in short, every other peculiar to the forest, here attain a growth seldom equalled and never surpassed in Europe ; while the box and the juniper rise to a height, and flourish with a luxuriance, almost incredible to an European.

In addition to these, the mulberry, chesnut, olive, pomegranate, indeed the whole of the fruit trees found in a favoured clime, grow wild, in the most abundant profusion ; we may also number among these the prickly pear, the sweet cherry, and the acid plum, so rarely met with in Europe.

These regions also produce the vine, hop, and every description of parasitical plant, twining from tree to tree, from peak to peak, forming the most delightful arbours. The red and almond-leaved willows, and creeping brambles of every species and shade, adorn the banks of the rivulets; gigantic thistles, with their many-coloured blossoms, burdock, wild orach, and various others, reach the highest perfection.

Even the sea coast is rich in the most interesting marine plants, such as the cheropodium-maritimum, the artemisia, statice limonium, atriplex

laciniata, amaranthus blitum, crambe orientalis,
particularly the statice coriaria, so valuable to the
tanner, this, together with the gall-nut, which
also abounds, and the bark of the white birch,
formed articles of lucrative commerce with
Turkey. The oil obtained from the inside rind
of the latter is not more highly prized by the
Turks than the bark in tanning. As this oil forms
a valuable addition to the pharmacopœia of the
eastern hakkim in the present day, on account of
its sanative qualities in the cure of wounds, it is
supposed by some Eastern writers to have been
the celebrated balsam used by Sultan Saladin
during the wars of the Crusaders.

Next to the majestic oak in importance, we
must place the wild cherry and linden ;* the

---

* Of every other tree connected with rural economy,
perhaps the linden is the most valuable. In Russia, its properties are so well understood that we see it growing in
every hamlet and village possessing a soil capable of nourishing it. The wood is not only manufactured into furniture ;
but into a variety of domestic utensils. Cords and matting
are made from its inner rind, while its aromatic blossoms not
only perfume the air and feed the bees, but make an agreeable tisane for the invalid ; at the same time, the young tender
sprigs, with their foliage, serve to mix with the fodder during
the depth of winter, being highly palatable to the cattle. I have
already, in my previous works, more than once alluded to this

latter is highly useful to the Circassians, for the
bees, after feeding on its blossoms, produce the
fine green honey, aromatic in odour and delicious
in flavour, esteemed so great a delicacy by the
rich gourmands of Constantinople and Teheran.
In order to ensure its good qualities, the honey is
removed from the hive previously to the blossom
changing its colour. The pine, and other trees
that flourish on the lofty heights of Europe, are
here rarely met with, even in the highest situations; but bilberries, wortleberries, raspberries,
black currants, cranberries, and several species
of strawberries, grow plentifully on the hills and
among the rich herbage of the slopes and terraces.

The aspect of these elevated ridges, vernal to
the summit, is beautiful beyond description : intermingled with the wide-spreading forest trees of
every species, we see the varied shrubs of dwarf
plane trees, dwarf elms, down to the poplar, willow and alder, that skirt the meandering rivulets.
In addition to these, the pomegranate, the varied
fruit of the mulberry, black, white, and violet,

very useful tree, with a desire to promote its cultivation in
our own country; for, independent of its utility, it is ornamental, and may be seen adorning nearly every public garden
and promenade in Germany.

together with numerous others, form a luxuriant picture, rarely seen out of the Caucasus.

Besides the number of rare plants, so interesting to the botanist, those adapted to culinary purposes are numerous, particularly the rhubarb and a species of horse radish, which are every where found growing wild; the latter plant, which the natives call batergan, is so immense in size as to resemble a small tree; the root frequently attains six inches in diameter and a yard in length; it is eaten with meat, made up in a sauce; and if it does not possess the pungency of our own, it has this advantage, that its flowers when boiled are not inferior to brocoli. Wild carrots, turnips, gourds, onions, melons, and cucumbers, are also included in their vegetables. To these we may add another, to which I must give the German name *kohl rüben* (turnip cabbage), the cultivation of which in England might, I think, be highly advantageous; and as it has found its way from South Russia, and now abounds in some parts of Germany, there can be nothing in our climate to prevent its growth; and partaking, as it does, of the qualities of both turnip and cabbage, it could not fail of becoming deservedly popular.

From the peculiarly fine flavour of the cucumber

and the various species of melons, each surpassing the other in excellence, it would appear as if they were indigenous to this part of the Caucasus; but however gratifying to the taste, indulgence in them is certain of producing fever, more especially to the stranger. Of water melons, the best kind and most wholesome is that with a dark red pulp and very small seed. The fruit of the solanum melongia, so frequently found in Asia, is here much cultivated; it is generally fried in butter, and eaten with meat.

Vast quantities of the common rhododendron, the rhododendron-caucasicum, and the azalia-pontica, grow on the loftier situations; and, as I before remarked, great attention being paid to the cultivation of bees, the blossoms of these plants are much valued, for they impart to the honey that singular intoxicating quality mentioned by Xenophon, Strabo, and other ancient writers. Even a small quantity of this honey mixed with mead forms a beverage possessing the power to inebriate in an equal degree with the strongest spirituous liquors.

The Cossacks inhabiting the banks of the Kouban, who, like the Russian boors, are not celebrated for sobriety, evince for it so strong a predilection, that, in order to obtain it, they will not hesitate to barter with the Circassians the very powder that may be instrumental in their own destruction.

Perhaps no other people bestow more attention on the husbandry of their bees than the mountaineers of the Caucasus; and the quantity of honey they obtain is really extraordinary.; this, with the wax, formed the principal articles of commerce of these poor people with Turkey and the neighbouring countries previous to the blockade of the coast by Russia.

The common honey is of a pale yellow colour, and, like the other sorts I have alluded to, most agreeable in its flavour. There is also a species of wild honey found in the clefts of the rocks in Upper Abasia, so perfectly indurated, that it is necessary to dissolve it in water preparatory to using it. This honey is a favourite article with the Circassian in his guerilla expeditions. Whether this peculiar hardness was natural to the honey, or produced by some artificial process, I am unable to determine; it has a pleasant spicy taste, is perfectly white, and may be preserved for years, except that it becomes yellow from age, and, instead of being viscous, is brittle, like sugar-candy.

Apricots, apples, and other dried fruits, are also much used in the camp, and, when boiled in a syrup of honey and wine, are deservedly popular with these people.

The vine is much cultivated in this province. In addition to the white wines, somewhat resembling in flavour those of the neighbourhood of Rome, they make another wine, from the common black wild grape, more spirituous in its nature; when making the latter, they are accustomed to mix with the new wine, (which is always boiled,) honey, together with the juice of raisins and blackberries.

Although the province of Khapsoukhie, from the contiguity of its mountains to the Black Sea, possesses no river of importance, it is everywhere intersected by meandering streams, among which the Bakan, Zemes, Apin, Bugunder, and the Antihir, are the most considerable. These flow onward, for the most part, to the Black Sea, (or become tributary to the minor rivers that empty their waters into the Kouban,) through deep defiles, glens, and chasms, which, constituting the prevailing features of the country, and being in a manner the barrier of defence to the tribes in the interior, we cannot feel surprised that the inha-

bitants, thus intrenched in their inaccessible fastnesses, have hitherto bid defiance to every effort
of Russia to subdue them. Year after year numerous forces, supplied with all the *materiel* of
war, have vainly attempted to possess themselves
of these mountain fortifications.

The Khapsoukhians, notwithstanding their
country is exceedingly fertile, do not pursue agriculture as might be expected, merely contenting
themselves with cultivating as much millet, maize,
buck-wheat, barley, and rice, as will suffice for
their own consumption, preferring the less labo-
rious and to them more interesting employment
of tending their flocks and herds.

The horned cattle are of a small size, similar
to those I have seen on the south coast of the
Crimea; they employ them instead of the buffalo,
as we see in the opposite coast of Anadolia, in
drawing their two-wheeled carts. It is really
astonishing to see how rapidly these animals pass
over the high hills, impeded by the entangled
brushwood; for in the whole of Circassia there is
nothing in the shape of a road, unless we so term
the bed of some dried-up river or rivulet.

The structure of these carts, which are peculiar to the Caucasus, is so extremely singular, that

they must be as primitive in their design as those
used by King Priam during the siege of Troy.
The Circassians, however, merely employ them
for carrying the produce of the field in harvest-
time, as both men and women of every rank
journey on horseback. It is true, these carts are
awkward-looking vehicles ; still the way in which
they are constructed affords considerable facility
in their transportation, the friction being confined to the ground and the axletree, as the wheels
do not turn round on the axle, but the axle re-
volves with them. The wheels, of which there
are only two to each cart, are not composed of
spokes, but hewn out of one solid piece of wood ;
and, as the vehicle is made without a particle of
iron, and never greased, the music, heard far and
wide over the distant hills, is anything but har-
monious.

The sheep, principally of the long-tailed race, are
excellent, and produce a fine wool, while the flavour
of the meat is equal to that of the best South Down
of our own country ; from the wool they manufacture a good kind of cloth, while the black and
coarser wool, with the long hair of the goats, are
used in making their inimitable cloaks. The women are all weavers. They also spin from the wild

hemp, a plant which frequently attains the height of ten feet, a very good kind of yarn, which is said to excel that produced from the cultivated plant in strength and durability. Since the interruption of their commerce by Russia, the want of an outlet for these articles, which they formerly exported in large quantities to Turkey and the Crimea, has entailed many privations upon these industrious people. The same interruption has deprived them of salt, a want which has been severely felt, the mortality being very great among their cattle, particularly the sheep, unless they are plentifully supplied with this article, or some other efficient substitute.

Russia, well knowing the importance of salt to the mountaineers, not contented with blockading their coast, and thereby depriving them of the supply they were accustomed to receive from Turkey, appropriated by force the saline springs near the Wladi-Kaukas, to which those who lived at a distance from the Euxine were accustomed to drive their cattle, this being one of the means by which she proposed to reduce these people to subjection.

Man, however primitive, however uninformed, is fruitful in invention, and the Circassians have now ascertained that a plentiful supply of lye, mixed with the food of their cattle, answers, in some degree, the purposes of salt ; while for seasoning their own viands, when that article cannot be obtained, they are obliged to be contented with sour milk, honey, and capsicums. That these substitutes will not impart an agreeable flavour to some dishes cannot be denied ; but on the health of the people, the want of salt does not appear to have been injurious, as nothing could have been more robust or vigorous than the general appearance of the population.

CHAPTER XVII.

Abasian horses—Attention paid to breeding them—Penalty
of falsifying their lineage—Training—Poultry—Extraordinary fertility of the soil—Forests—Excellence of the
timber—Game—The Caucasian partridge—Fish—Character of the people—Their armour—Form of government— Chiefs and elders —Domestic administration—
Circassian knights—Their character.

PERHAPS to no part of their domestic economy
do the Abasian people, and indeed the Circassians in general, bestow so much attention as to
breeding horses, the qualities of that noble animal being as well understood, its excellence as
highly appreciated, as much attention paid to its
treatment, and the genealogy of the different
races as familiar to them, as if they were fre-
quenters of Newmarket, or Arabs of the desert.
Each race has its own peculiar mark branded on
the haunch.

The different genealogies being transmitted from father to son, if any deceit is practised, such as endeavouring to impose a horse of inferior lineage for one of noble, the perpetrator is summoned before a council of the elders, tried, and punished, by the imposition of heavy fines, be his rank what it may ; for of nothing are these people so tenacious as the preservation of a good breed of horses. We cannot feel surprised at this, when we remember how often the life of a Circassian depends upon the swiftness of his horse. It is not only beauty of form, but fleetness and durability, that is regarded in the selection of the breed. They train them to endure hunger and fatigue, to swimming, and all the other accomplishments and qualifications requisite for the companion of a guerilla warrior ; and in docility and tractableness the Circassian horses are surpassed by none.

The most celebrated race in the Caucasus, termed Shalokh, is preserved, in all its purity, by a Tartar prince, whose family has been domiciliated for nearly a century in the highest range of the Black mountains : he is known by the name of the Tau-sultan, (mountain prince.) A horseshoe is the mark by which this splendid race of horses are distinguished, which, for beauty of form, strength of limb, and fleetness, cannot be surpassed by that of any country whatever. They more resemble the English racer than the Arabian horse of the desert, always command the most extravagant prices in Turkey and Persia, and are highly prized in Russia. In addition to those of a native breed, they possess some of the finest Persian and Arabian. Those which are most highly valued are distinguished by their separate genealogical marks.

The other domestic animals are those common to Europe; the poultry, such as chickens, ducks, geese, Indian fowls, &c., are all excellent of their kind. In fact, the entire province, and the greater part of the Western Caucasus, abounds with every requisite for the maintenance of a large population; there are meadows and pastures on the banks of the rivulets,—prairies and mountain plateaus; while the sunny slopes and various other fertile spots are capable of being converted into the finest arable land. Indeed, such is the productiveness of the soil, I have been assured, by several Poles and Russians domiciliated among the Circassians, that barley, millet, and wheat, yield an increase of upwards of thirteen fold, on an average. The corn in favoured situations is ready for the sickle in June, and this notwithstanding the very little attention bestowed on agriculture. Like the Tartars of the Crimea, the Circassians tread out the grain in the open fields with horses.

In addition to the fertility of the soil, the splendid forests could supply sufficient timber for all the purposes of commerce, together with fuel for ages; the box alone is so abundant, and of such gigantic proportions, as to ensure a very extensive trade. Game is everywhere plentiful; the majestic stag, the roebuck, and the deer, descend from the mountains; the wild boar, porcupine, and hares, are everywhere met with. Wild-fowl are also abundant; the pheasant and the turkey are natives of the Caucasus. The cock of the wood, bustards, woodcocks, together with every other bird of passage, abound in their season. The Caucasian partridge is spread over the whole country; this fine bird, although it resembles the European one in form, is nearly as large as a capon. Trout, shad, perch, pike, tench, and every other species of the finny tribe peculiar to mountain streams, are here in the greatest profusion, and of the most delicious flavour.

The Khapsoukhians, as well as the other Circassian tribes among whom I mingled, are lively, communicative, polite, and officious,—cleanly in their houses and persons, much attached to ornamental dress, and the possession of splendid arms and fine horses, and may be said, considering the war and the unsettled state of the country, to be a prosperous people, their wants being few, and their manner of living simple. They never leave the limits of their homesteads or hamlets without being completely armed, and their breast pockets filled with ball-cartridges. Their visits of ceremony are usually made in a coat of mail; one of a lighter description, bullet-proof, is generally worn under their clothes on the most ordinary occasions.*

* The armour generally worn by the Circassians consists of helmets, cuirasses, and cuises, composed of small steel plates laid over each other, and so contrived as not to impede the motion of the body; the cuirass is usually lined with woollen stuff. The chain armour of the ancient Persians is also frequently adopted; the helmets resemble those of antiquity, and are so made as to protect the neck and fasten under the chin, after the manner of the knights of the middle ages. Their swords and daggers exceed in temper and workmanship the finest productions of Great Britain; some of these, together with the armour, are preserved in families from time immemorial.

The Khapsoukhie tribes have no hereditary princes or chiefs ; the man who is the most powerful from family alliances, and is at the same time brave in the field and wise in council, being selected as their military leader.

On account of the insecurity of the country, from war and other causes, there is not a single town, nor even what we would term a village, throughout the whole province, the inhabitants dwelling in hamlets, or homesteads. On invasion, defeat, or the approach of an enemy, they demolish their little habitations, and transport their household furniture and valuable effects to some secure situation, setting fire to the remainder.

In these hamlets the houses are built contiguous to each other, in the form of a circle or square, the inner space serving as an inclosure for their cattle during the depth of winter. The dwelling of the chief, Usden, or Mourza, (who is the presiding magistrate, and always a man of substance,) is detached from the hamlet ; and, as his rank and long-established custom obliges him to accommodate the stranger, and maintain dependents and slaves about his person, his residence is composed of several cots, forming in themselves a hamlet.

Besides these houses, the Circassians are accustomed to dig large pits in the forest or some
such remote place, to serve as a retreat to the
aged, women, and children, in case of being taken
by surprise. These pits are neatly fitted up,
being lined with wicker-work made of oziers,
or some such pliable material; and, as they are
ingeniously covered over, an enemy rarely dis-
covers them. The Circassians, in their selection
of a spot to settle in, always choose the banks of
a river or rivulet; when this cannot be found,
they conduct water to their hamlets from some
neighbouring rivulet by means of canals; in lieu
of a better material, they use the trunks of decayed
trees for that purpose.

The priests and elders, who are much respected,
are generally distinguished by a red turban and a
flowing beard—the badge of wisdom. In addition
to these, there are several Usdens (noblemen), a
species of lord of the manor, who frequently exercise the calling of priest, elder, and magistrate.
Their influence is very considerable among the
peasantry, from whom they exact a trifling tribute,
consisting of a few days' work on their farms, the
customary presents of cattle on marriage and other
festive occasions, together with the stipulated

allowance of sheep, grain, &c., for the subsistence
of their military followers during the summer
encampment, and in some measure to cover the
expenses they incur in keeping open house for the
reception of strangers. These contributions are
regularly levied upon each householder at a general assembly of the elders.

The power of the military chiefs here, as elsewhere in the Western Caucasus, is very considerable, and their influence extensive; but that
office being elective, it is their interest, not only
to attach the affection of their clansmen, but to
command their admiration by every act of generosity and daring valour,—virtues considered by
these people as inherent in every man of gentle
blood, any deviation from which would only entail upon them universal contempt, and subject
them to the imputation of being aliens to the blood
of the noble race to which they might happen to
belong, besides the loss of their command as
leaders in time of war, and the deprivation of the
honour of being foremost in the chace. Hence a
Circassian knight is rarely tyrannical in the exercise of his authority, and none among his followers more renowned for bravery, generosity,
and expertness in the chace.

So little changed is the character of the Circassian knight for generosity and noble feeling, that the description given by Signor Interiano, the famous Genoese traveller, in the fourteenth century, is equally applicable in the nineteenth. We will therefore quote the character he has given us of the Circassian knight of that day, in his own quaint phraseology.

" The Circassian knight is a great admirer of generosity, and cheerfully gives away everything he possesses, except his horse and arms. In respect to his apparel, he is not only liberal, but profuse ; hence he cuts a worse figure in this respect than his own vassals. Whenever he puts on new clothes, or a shirt of crimson silk, a vassal frequently begs them as a present ; it would be deemed the greatest disgrace if he denied or seemed unwilling to comply with such a request. If, therefore, any one solicits the gift of the clothes upon their back, they immediately pull them off, and change them for those of the meanest applicant, be he ever so squalid. Thus the nobles and knights are almost always worse equipped than the common people, except in regard to boots, arms, and horses, which they never part with, and in which their chief pride consists.

" They often give all their moveable property for a fine horse to which they may take a fancy; and there is nothing in the whole world they prize so highly as an excellent horse. When they get possession of gold or silver, either by predatory violence or in any other manner, they spend it immediately in the purchase of horses and military equipments."

The same writer, in speaking of the Circassians, says, that " they are in general well-shaped and handsome, among whom are to be found figures of uncommon symmetry. The same remark is applicable to the women; they fulfil all the duties of hospitality with the most scrupulous attention, and both the host and guest style each other ' konak,' which is synonimous with ' hospes' in Latin."

We will now proceed with our own account. In conformity with the feudal institutions of these people—by which I mean the whole of the Circassian tribes—every man capable of bearing arms, particularly if he has any pretensions to nobility or knighthood, is bound to follow his chief to the field, cowardice being considered, of all others, the greatest crime, and none punished with such severity, or treated with such unmea-

sured contempt : the noble who should exhibit
the slightest symptom of fear or wavering resolution on the day of battle would be instantly
deprived of his dignity and everything he possessed. With such laws and institutions, can we
wonder at the bravery of these people, and the
difficulties Russia has to surmount before she
can succeed in subjugating them?

CHAPTER XVIII.

Excursion to the bay of Djook—Effects of Russian devastation — Coast of Upper Abasia — Superb forests — Luxuriant vegetation—The Caucasian raven—Tomb of a Circassian chief—Bay of Djook—Anchorage—Repeated attempts of the Russians to take it—Their ill-success— Resolute determination of the mountaineers to defend it —Russian cannon.

WE remained for a day the guests of Prince Mahmood, during which time I was extremely fortunate in meeting with my young friend Beitzrouku, from whom I received so much kindness on my first arrival in the Caucasus, and who was now on his way to Constantinople, being deputed by the confederated chiefs to carry thither the account of the victories of the Circassians, and to make arrangements with the Turkish merchants for procuring ammunition, and various other articles, necessary for carrying on the ensuing campaign.

My konak, and several other chieftains, being also on their way to Abasia, and the other eastern provinces of the Caucasus, with the intention of animating their compatriots in those provinces, and strengthening the confederacy by forming alliances with the principal leaders and elders, I felicitated myself not a little in having so many gallant warriors as my companions, by which means I should be secure of their protection, instead of relying on the good faith of the inhabitants during my journey to the bay of Djook, where I expected to find the captain of the vessel in which I arrived in Circassia; who, after taking in part of his cargo at Pchad, was to remain in the bay of Djook till I should join him. Thus provided with so sufficient an escort, and having previously obtained the emancipation of my servant Nathan, before alluded to, who was most anxious to accompany me to Europe, together with the prospect of gleaning much information relative to the Circassian province of Abasia, I promised myself a pleasant excursion, in which I was not disappointed.

We journeyed along the sea coast to Djook: the weather was delightful, a temperature at once balmy to the feelings and bracing to the frame having suc-

ceeded the great heats of summer and autumn.
The splendid Euxine, like an expansive lake, lay
spread out before us in all its loveliness, still agi-
tated in waving billows, the effects of the late hurricane. But how desolate, how dreary! On that
vast expanse not a single sail was to be seen, not
even the tiny skippers of the Turks. The Russian cruisers, however strict in guarding the coast,
had also disappeared, so violent had been the late
winds.

The prospect along the coast was not less
dreary. The pretty cots, surrounded with their
flocks and herds, that only a few months previous
adorned these vast and fertile hills, and which I
had so much admired while coasting, now presented so many blackened ruins; no song of the
shepherd, no cry of the huntsman, not even the
unharmonious creaking of the mountain-car now
greeted my ear, the tramp of our own horses
being the only sounds that interrupted the awful
stillness which reigned in the deep defiles and
narrow glens, the unfortunate natives having
been obliged to retire into the interior at some
distance from the coast, on account of the increasing persecutions they had been subjected to.
In short, the desolation was so appalling, so differ-

ent from every other country in the neighbourhood
of civilized Europe, that, were it not for the remaining traces of the inhabitants, it might have
been deemed a region unknown—uninhabited.

Such were the effects of the devastating and
harassing war, originating with the civilized court
of St. Petersburg, a government that pretends to
be guided in its councils by humanity, by a desire
to promote the prosperity of nations, the advance-
ment of civilization, and a determination to support with its influence every existing power established in consonance with the recognised laws of
nations.   Yet how inconsistent is the policy of
Russia ! how insatiable her thirst for dominion !
We see her at the same time squandering millions
of roubles, year after year, in replenishing the
empty coffers of the pretender in Spain, and
draining her treasury in endeavouring to subjugate a free independent people.   Let him that
doubts the aggressive, aye, the revolutionary, de-
moralizing policy of Russia, if he has not courage
to dare the danger of a Russian blockade, (after
all, more ideal than real,) and visit Circassia,
wander through Turkey, follow any one of her
numerous revolutionary agents, not only in that
country, but in Persia, Central Asia, and indeed

in every part of Europe, to be satisfied of the
necessity of coercing the measures of a government so unprincipled, so Machiavelian, unless
we would speedily see the world a prey to all the
horrors of another twenty years' war.

These luxuriant mountains, where only a few
years since numerous flocks and herds gamboled
among the rich herbage in peaceful security,
where a happy people enjoyed all the comforts of
rural life, and carried on a flourishing commerce
with their neighbours, the Turks and Persians,
are now a mere desert, the abode of the soaring
eagle, the rapacious vulture, the prowling wolf,
the melancholy owl, and the pelican of the wil-
derness. Like the dog in the manger, Russia,
knowing that she cannot appropriate the country
to herself, owing to the near approach of the
glens and defiles to the coast, and the facility
they offer as an ambuscade to the mountaineers
to exterminate her legions, has determined to
reduce it to a desert, and well has she succeeded
in her attempt; for the few natives that joined
our escort related, with tears in their eyes, a distressing account of the incessant persecutions and
losses they sustained during the summer and
autumn from the Russian blockade vessels, whose

crew of plunderers, whenever they perceive the slightest chance of making a successful predatory incursion, never fail to land and carry off every thing within their reach.

During my ride, I found the same plants, the same trees, the same luxuriant herbage I before alluded to. Wherever I turned my eyes I discovered the most magnificent oak in these virgin forests; here torn down by the tempest, there decaying from extreme age: even the box and juniper, dwarf shrubs in Europe, kept pace in magnitude with the colossal oak.

Intermingled with the common grass, the stipapennata (feather-grass) and various other tufted grasses, so gigantic in size and height, and for the most part strangers in Europe, here everywhere abound. These grasses are considered highly nutritious for cattle, particularly horses, who feed on them with avidity. The most common plants of the meadow and favoured situations were the luxuriant rheum-caspium (wild rhubarb), prodigious in size; the colchicum autumnale (meadow saffron), so celebrated in the cure of gout and rheumatism; the phaseolus radiatus, together with tulips, and other flowers, without end, and of every variety. While the azalea pontica, the clematis orientalis, and numerous other shrubs and parasitical plants, not less beautiful than rare, seem to derive their only nourishment from the flinty rock. Among these, and through the long grass, the grillas tataricus and oxycephalus, with swarms of beautiful insects, of every shade and hue, disported with delight.

The banks of the little rivulets were here and there shaded with the wide-spreading branches of the tamarisk, and numerous shrubs of the liquorice species; the roots of these shrubs, together with the wild rhubarb and saffron, and even the reeds* of the marshes, were formerly much in demand by the Turks, hundreds of peasants being employed in collecting them.

The land tortoise was so numerous in this land of nature as to be frequently crushed under our horses' feet; the pretty curled-tailed lizard, in its manifold shades, so rare in most countries, was here as plentiful as the grasshopper in our own meadows; and the porcupine crossed our path as frequently as hares. Scorpions, of every species, and serpents, of immense size, with the scolo-

* The Caucasian reed is much in demand by the Turks and Persians, it being considered preferable to their own for writing, these people rarely using the quill for that purpose.

pendra morsitans, phalangium araneoïdes, were
also more abundant than could have been wished
for ; and here I saw, for the first time, the Caucasian raven, with its dark red legs and scarlet bill.

These vast hills, which still retain the name of
the Black Mountains, appeared to rise in altitude
as we advanced, and to form the base of the
great Caucasian range, glimpses of which we occasionally caught, towering to the heavens in all
their wintry grandeur. They were principally
composed of a calcareous substance, and but
seldom porous or petrified; sometimes a ridge,
however, shewed evident marks of a volcano ;
and not far from Djook there is a glen, like the
Grotta del Cane, at Naples, said to be so full of
mephitic air as to endanger the lives of those
whose temerity might lead them to enter it.

This beautiful and highly-favoured district has
also the advantage of being admirably irrigated,
so much so that scarcely the length of a mile in-
tervenes before you come to a tiny valley, with a
stream of water meandering to the coast. We
encamped for a few hours on the bank of one of
these rivulets, near the tomb of a Circassian
chieftain, who fell in a skirmish with the Russians
about a year ago. He must have been a man of

no little influence and celebrity, for every one of
the party shewed their grief by beating their fore-
heads with their whips,—a practice I before observed to be prevalent among these people. The
tomb, erected upon a projecting eminence, was
rudely constructed of stone, in the form of an
oblong square, each corner being adorned with a
post, surmounted by a carved head.

During the time my companions occupied themselves praying for the soul of the deceased in a
sacred grove contiguous, I amused myself in
botanizing, and admiring the beautiful varieties
of pebbles in the bed of the rivulet; among many
others, the black basalt, the brown, green, white,
and black porphyry, the red, white, and grey
granite, predominated, and I even observed some
specimens of the verd antique and lapis lazuli;
but in all my researches I was not so fortunate as
to find rubies or diamonds.

We were occupied full eight hours in riding
from Pchad to Djook; but how great was our
mortification, on arriving in that bay, to find
that the captain of our vessel had sailed for Trebizond a week previous, owing to the violence of
the winds, and the insecurity of Djook as a harbour. He, however, left word with one of the

chiefs of the district, that, as soon as he had discharged his cargo at Trebizond, we might depend upon his returning, with his vessel re-laden, to one of the little Turkish ports in Lazestahn, where he would await our arrival, weather permitting. Provided, as I was, with a safe escort, and pleasant companions, the departure of the vessel was no cause of vexation, as it afforded me an opportunity of seeing more of the country.

The semicircular form of the bay of Djook, with the surrounding hills, gives it a very picturesque appearance ; but owing to its being exposed to the violence of the land winds in spring and autumn, it cannot be considered a secure harbour.

The Russians have made several ineffectual attempts to possess themselves of the bay of Djook, not only this year, but nearly every year since the treaty of Adrianople, on account of it being a favourite rendezvous of the Turkish traders, who are accustomed to supply the mountaineers with salt and powder. Their little vessels can always ride securely in some nook or other of the bay, however much the violence of the wind might endanger a large vessel.

As the military chief of this district was not

yet returned from the camp of his ally, the
Demirghoi chieftain, we took up our quarters at
the house of Ismaelbeg, an elder and high priest,
it being contrary to etiquette among these people
to enter the house of any Circassian in the
absence of its master.

The country inland from Djook is exceedingly
populous. I was much pleased with the various
clusters of houses scattered in different direc-
tions, like so many separate villages, each cluster
being surrounded with a strong fence, together
with cultivated fields, looking like so many little
parks ; indeed, every spot among the luxuriant
forest trees, now so beautifully variegated with
the rich tints of autumn, exhibited signs of the
labours of the husbandman. Numerous herds of
cattle and an admirable race of horses browzed
upon the surrounding hills, whose graceful forms
added their full share in giving animation and
picturesque effect to a landscape replete with
every feature that could charm the eye and please
the imagination. It was indeed a glorious picture, and the more delightful from its contrast
with the melancholy scene through which I had
passed while travelling along the coast. Yet
these are the people whom their enemies repre-

sent as a migratory race, living in tents like
Arabs and gypsies, and following no other occupations than tending their flocks and herds, and
plundering their neighbours.

That the inhabitants of this district still continue to enjoy in peace their patrimonial fields,
is owing to their own bravery, and perhaps more
than all to the natural strength of the narrow
valleys, which may be said to form so many inaccessible defiles down to the sea coast.

Notwithstanding all the disadvantages of
Djook as a harbour, it is quite as famous as
Soudjook-Kalé in the annals of Circassian victories ; so much so, that nearly every family in
the neighbouring hamlets possess some trophy
of the defeat of the invaders. Only the year
previous to my visit, they captured several pieces
of cannon, and cut to pieces from between two to
three thousand Russians, who had the temerity
to advance into the interior.

Our host, Islambeg, introduced to our notice
several of these Russian guns ; they are kept in
capital order, and well mounted ; he also shewed
us an immense heap of stone balls, with which he
said his compatriots were determined to give the
enemy a warm reception on their next visit,—for

these people, owing to their constant intercourse with the Turks of Armenia and Anadolia on the opposite coast, are well supplied with gunpowder and salt, for which they give them tallow, wax, honey, and corn, in return ; in short, the inhabitants of this district, with the exception of the landholders residing near the coast, have not yet experienced any serious ill effects from the blockade which has so materially inconvenienced those provinces of Circassia through which I had so recently travelled.

CHAPTER XIX.

Departure from Djook—Gratitude of the Circassians to-
    wards their warriors—Hospitality of the people—Super-
    stition of the mountaineers of Abasia—Astrologers—
    Moral qualities of the people—Gloomy defile of Jagra
    —Russian fortress—Bay of Vadran—Log-houses of the
    Russian troops—Their destruction—Violent hostility of
    the Tartars settled in Abasia to Russia—Tartar sultans
    —Their ferocious appearance—Deplorable state of the
    garrison at Vadran—Demolition of ancient churches in
    Abasia—Causes which produced it.

On leaving Djook, it was really delightful to
witness the kind attention of this interesting
people, for on merely mentioning our wish for a
change of horses, numbers of the natives flew to
the hills to procure them, and those whose horses
we selected considered themselves most highly
honoured ; such is the enthusiasm in favour of the
warrior whose efforts and toils are devoted to the
defence of his country, that no sacrifice is deemed
too great, no compensation too precious, to re-

ward the man who voluntarily exerts himself to repel the enemy that would enslave the land of his birth.

In addition to a plentiful entertainment provided by our host, the women of the neighbouring hamlets were equally forward in giving us a hospitable reception ; they made small packages, containing the choicest productions of the dairy and the bees, together with dried fruits and fresh-baked barley cakes, which were secured to our saddles, that we might not want provisions on our route. As to meat and poultry, and other good things, so necessary to the maintenance of a traveller in Europe, a Circassian rarely makes use of them during an excursion ; the evening meal is that in which they most indulge ; but should he at any time feel desirous to enjoy such a luxury, so long as a fat buck bounds through his native hills, or a pheasant or turkey wings its way through the air, he is certain of a plentiful repast, for the Circassians are universally good marksmen. Besides, every homestead, according to ancient usage, is obliged to furnish a chief, on his excursion, who is at peace with their tribe, a sheep and other provisions.

Being determined to attempt procuring, at

Soutchali, Ardler, or some of the other little bays on the coast, a vessel to convey us to Trebizond, we set forward, accompanied as usual for a few miles by hundreds of the inhabitants, singing in full chorus their warlike songs; there were also among them a few wandering minstrels, who, acccording to custom, chanted the praise and gallant deeds of each individual warrior; in addition to these there were saints, soothsayers, and astrologers, to predict a happy termination to our long journey; for no people are more superstitious, none more prone to put their faith in every species of spell and charm, than the Caucasians, particularly the inhabitants of Upper Abasia,* which commences at Djook.

The most common form of divination I observed, and which was repeatedly practised during our stay at Djook, was to take a handful of barleycorns, made up of some specific number, but which I now forget, and then divide them into seven small heaps, placed at certain distances

---

* Strictly speaking, it is only Upper Abasia that can be called the country of the Abasians; for the whole of that part of the coast termed in the map Lower Abasia, and which, commencing at Djook, extends to the Kouban, is inhabited by tribes more or less of Attéghéi lineage.

from each other, and according to fixed rules; they are then counted, and the corresponding numbers supposed to predict the failure or success of the enterprise about to be commenced. It was really ludicrous to observe the solemn countenances of my konak and the other elders and chiefs during the time the astrologer was reading the fate of their journey, convinced as they no doubt were of the infallibility of the augury. But when the little magic corns announced to me an unpropitious termination to my own tour home, nothing could exceed their vexation and anxiety.

Such, indeed, is their implicit belief in these unmeaning spells, that few will undertake any important enterprise when their horoscope is clouded by gloomy forebodings; consequently, they unanimously joined in entreating me to remain for a few days till the good Spirit should be propitiated by prayer and sacrifice. Another very common charm was, to throw the blade-bone of a shoulder of mutton into the fire, when the number of cracks produced, and the direction to which they point, whether east, west, north or south, is supposed to indicate with certainty the fate of an enterprise.

In addition to these, the various changes of the moon, and the aspect of the stars, are also consulted. Certain birds, or animals that may cross their path during a journey, together with such persons first met on leaving home, who may be blessed or cursed with particular coloured eyes and hair, are all omens of good or evil; and as all these, and many others, influence the decision of a Circassian in any work he may be about to commence, we must wonder, when we take into account the difficulty of finding all these indexes of fortune pointing at the same moment to success, that he undertakes any dangerous enterprise.

Still this superstitious belief has one good effect upon a people of such enthusiastic and sanguine temperament, for should the omen be found propitious they enter upon their task with an alacrity and confidence that almost ensures success from the vigour it imparts to their efforts.

The degrading superstition of these mountaineers must, however, appear inevitable, when we remember that, owing to the inaccessible nature of their mountain fastnesses, and their jealousy and suspicion of foreigners, they have been, from time immemorial, shut out from the

slightest ray of European intelligence. Must we
not, then, admire the civilization and morality at
which they have arrived, and that without any
written law—any other guide than the traditions
of their forefathers and the songs of their bards?
In truth, it is no exaggeration to say, that these
children of nature practise virtues which would
do honour to the most civilized nations of Europe.
Take, for instance, their respect and veneration
for age, — their courteous behaviour towards
women, however low may be their rank in life.
The man enfeebled by declining years, instead of
becoming an object of scorn and contempt to
thoughtless youth, as is, unhappily, too often seen
in Europe, is here respected and venerated by all
classes of society. Wherever he moves, the crowd
opens a path to his progress; all the little atten-
tions that a kind people are capable of exercising
are certain to be his. In winter, the warmest
corner of the fire is assigned; in summer, his
cushion is arranged under the shade of the
veranda, while the beautiful hands of his lovely
daughter are employed in fanning away the insects that might disturb his repose; presents of
sweetmeats, and all the little delicacies usually
given to children in other countries, are bestowed

upon him. In short, they act fully up to their own proverb—"Doubly accursed is the man that draweth down upon himself the curse of the aged."

With regard to the respect paid to women, I have frequently seen the gallant chief of thousands of warriors descend from his charger, and place on it some lonely damsel who might be trudging along through the deep valleys to visit a distant friend, and protect her safely to the next hamlet. At any time, a noble knight would consider himself disgraced were he to pass a woman without offering his services to defend her from danger and insult.

Let us contrast this conduct of the Circassian with that of too many of the European knights of the middle ages, with their immorality, their excesses, their barbarities, and we must esteem this gallant, simple-minded people, and feel assured that, if they were enlightened with the divine truths of Christianity, they will one day become an ornament to human nature.

Owing to the circumstance of the little bay of Vadran, about twenty miles distant from Djook, being in possession of the Russians, we were obliged, after an hour's ride, to leave the coast, and take an inland direction towards the defile of Jagra. This famous pass, with its towering crags and masses of black limestone rock and slate, might be supposed to resemble the entrance to Tartarus. The great height of the rocks, and the thick foliage of the lofty trees, by which it is overhung, renders the gorge, for the most part, impervious to the sun, except during an hour or two at mid-day; while, to add to its horrors, a roaring rivulet is seen in the dark abyss dashing with rapidity over the broken rocks that form its bed.

This defile, one of the strongest in the country, is said to communicate with most of the other defiles and valleys in the Western Caucasus; hence the Russian government have been most anxious to obtain possession of it. Every effort of its armies has, however, hitherto been ineffectual to penetrate beyond the ruins of a Genoese church and convent on the coast, which have been put into such state of defence as to resist the efforts of the mountaineers to chase away their disagreeable neighbours, unsupplied as they are with the necessary *materiel* of war.

Perhaps, of all the settlements of Russia on the coast of the Black Sea, that at Vadran has proved

the most destructive to her troops, both from the
hostility of the natives and the insalubrity of the
climate; for, being completely confined to their
contracted quarters, which are situated in the immediate neighbourhood of the defile, its damp
vapours and exhalations poison the whole atmosphere in its vicinity so long as the great heats of
summer and autumn continue.

Since my visit to Vadran, during the summer, several log-houses had been constructed for
the purpose of protecting the garrison from the
repeated attacks of the natives, or perhaps rather
to alarm them in case of any sudden and concerted
movement of the bands who are continually ho-
vering around them, and also, no doubt, with the
intention of affording a little more space for the
wretched soldiery of the garrison to extend their
promenade.

The object desired has not only not succeeded,
but has led to a still greater waste of life, for the
log-houses were no sooner constructed than they
were, for the most part, captured, and their in-
mates massacred, by the indefatigable mountaineers.

From the depth of the defile we ascended by
a circuitous path, flanked by high precipices, and

darkened by the thick foliage of the lofty trees, to the top of a high mountain, that so completely commands the fort of Vadran as to enable us to observe every movement of the soldiers in the garrison ; and any one who dared to advance beyond the precincts of some jutting parapet, erected to protect the sentinels from the bullets of the enemy, was certain of destruction. The garrison, having good reason to be on its guard against the murderous hostility of the neighbouring tribes, station sentinels, night and day, on the summit of the ruined tower of the church, defended by a breastwork, expressly for the purpose of giving alarm on the slightest appearance of danger ; and we could now distinctly see the confusion that ensued on the appearance of about a dozen warriors. Notwithstanding all their precautions, these daring mountaineers contrive to elude their vigilance by lying concealed for days in the herbage, expressly for the purpose of satiating their vengeance by shooting the soldiers singly.

Indeed, so great has been the mortality from this source, united to the prevalence of virulent fevers, which continually sweep away the men, that the garrison must be relieved, or increased, at least every six months. We cannot, therefore, bring ourselves to believe, everything considered, that any other European power than Russia would thus lavishly destroy the lives of its subjects in attempting to hold a position which cannot, from its locality, under present circumstances, ensure any important advantage; besides being surrounded with a poisonous atmosphere that engenders disease, and exposed to the rifle of an enemy that never slumbers, the little bay of Vadran is a mere creek, and very insecure, from its bad anchorage and exposure to violent winds; and the very attempt of an army, however strong, however well provided, to penetrate any distance into the interior, which must be through the defile Jagra, would be the very height of madness. At every step they would have to combat against the hostility of tribes, perhaps, of every other in the Caucasus, the most rancorous, the most malignant,—tribes whose hostility Russia has already provoked, the settlement at Vadran being in the immediate vicinity of several Tartar tribes, refugees from Krim-Tartary and from the Kouban and Caspian steppes; this is also the country of the most ferocious of all the Circassia-Abasia tribes, the Tschegreh and Kassilbeg; and not far distant, at the foot of the snowy mountains, is

the home of the Tubæ and the Ubœkh, to whom
I before alluded. Most of these tribes are more
or less under the influence of Tartar sultans.

Whatever sentiment of humanity, whatever
feeling of the generous soldier, might find a place
in the breast of the gallant knight of true Circassian
lineage, appears to be utterly unknown to these
half savages ; revenge, murderous revenge, being
the only motive that actuates them, they would
with delight exterminate the whole Russian race,
and never either give quarter or make a prisoner.
Indeed, the very aspect of these gigantic, ferocious
looking, ill-favoured Tartar sultans, in their sheep-
skin jackets and caps of long wool, which wave
wildly in the wind, the scymeter hanging by their
side, the long Greek gun slung across their shoulder, and pistols, poniard and hatchet stuck in their
broad silver belt, suggest to the imagination the
idea of an outlawed robber who had sworn eternal
enmity to civilized man. And however much we
may deprecate the policy of Russia, and regard her
encroachment in the Caucasus as an infringement of the laws and rights of nations, we
cannot but deplore the fate of her unhappy
soldiers serving in the Caucasus, particularly the
garrison at Vadran, exposed at once to the

inroads of disease and the bullets of these bandit
Tartars.   It would indeed be a charitable act to
transport a few field pieces to one of the commanding heights, and level to the earth the remains of the church and convent converted into a
fortress,—an achievement, from its ruined state,
that might be accomplished by a few hours' well
directed fire, and which, in the present state of
affairs in the Caucasus, would not be rebuilt.

Since the Russians have taken possession of
the old church and convent at Vadran, and fortified them, I have been assured that the Abasians
have destroyed several interesting remains of
antiquity, such as churches and convents of the
earliest Christians, under the apprehension that
the invaders might transform them into forts, and
thus enslave them.   This demolition is the more
to be regretted as there is every reason for believing that many contained records of high
value and great antiquity,—it being supposed,
from ancient manuscripts found in Armenia,
Mingrelia, and Georgia, that several of the tribes
inhabiting Abasia are descended from the early
Jews, converts to Christianity, who, being persecuted by their countrymen and the rulers of the
Roman empire, flew to the Caucasus, and there

settled,—an opinion strengthened by the circumstance that the features of several of these tribes
still bear the stamp of their Israelitish origin :
their religion to this day is a mixture of Judaism
and Christianity ; for instance, among other rites,
I have been assured that the feast of the passover
is celebrated with many of the ceremonies observed by the Jews when commemorating this
high festival.

CHAPTER XX.

Departure from Jagra—Route along the coast—Remains of
an ancient road—Attachment of the Circassians to England—Their desire to place themselves under its protection—Arrival at Soutchali—Hospitable reception by
an Usden—The Abasians a distinct race from the Circassians—Considered to be the aboriginal inhabitants of
the Western Caucasus—Their language totally distinct
from every other—Various dialects of the Caucasians.

HAVING got beyond the range of the Russian
guns at Vadran, we again continued our route
along the coast,—a route by far more agreeable
and less distressing to our horses, and I should
consider not much longer, with all its sinuosities,
than any other through the interior to Mingrelia,
when we take into consideration the time lost in
ascending and descending so many mountain
ridges, most of which in rainy weather are perfectly impassable for horses.　There is certainly
every appearance of an old road having been

carried from the Kouban, through the province
of Khapsoukhie, and which is said to continue
to Mingrelia and Imeritia, winding through the
valleys ; but this road being somewhat circuitous,
and a Circassian never making a detour, journeying on in defiance of all ordinary obstacles, we
did not pursue it for any length of time during
the excursions I made in the interior of the
country with my konak.

During our route along the coast, the mountains in some places approached so near to the sea
that the herbage and trees were washed with its
waves, in the same manner as if we were journeying along the banks of an inland lake. In
many places it was very evident that, at some
former period, a road had been actually carried
along this coast to Mingrelia, from the circumstance of the rocks being here and there cut
through by artificial means.

I know that one of the first measures of the
Russian government, when peaceable possession
of the country is obtained (!) will be to construct
a road along the coast to Mingrelia, which, if
ever completed, will be, in point of picturesque
scenery, one of the most beautiful over which a
traveller could pass ; but in the present situation

of affairs, even if that power had a road on this
coast, guarded by a chain of forts, it would not
be secure, owing to its being commanded by high
mountains, covered with impenetrable forests and
brushwood, which afford a safe ambush to the natives in their unwearied hostility against a power
they have so much reason to execrate.   Must we
not then feel convinced, from the localities of the
country, from the animosity of a whole people
towards the self-constituted authority of Russia,
that it would be her wisest course to retire from
a contest with some degree of honour before it is
too late,—some regard for the opinion of civilized
Europe, some semblance of humane feeling,
shall we say, of remorse for the multiplied evils
her aggressive policy and devastating arms are
inflicting upon the unoffending inhabitants of
these beautiful and fertile provinces—from a contest which must ever be a drain upon her treasury and population, so long as a forest and
a mountain remain in Circassia to serve as an
ambush and a fortification for her sons?

That the Circassians are desirous of forming a
stable government, and taking rank among those
of civilized nations, is evident from their repeated
offers to place themselves under the fostering care

of Great Britain ; and how proud ought we to be to find that not only do those persecuted for liberal opinions in Europe flee to us for protection, but that the oppressed even of Asia look towards us as the palladium of their hopes ; and how touching, how patriotic, how eloquent, is that passage in the declaration of independence of these poor people in which they allude to England!

" Let not," say the Circassians, " a great nation like England, to whom our eyes are turned and our hands are raised, think of us at all, if it be to do us injustice. Let her not open her ear to the wiles of the Russian, while she closes it to the prayer of the mountaineers of Circassia. Let her judge by facts, between a people called barbarous, and their calumniator!"

Again, say they, in the bold language of men determined to live or die independent—" We are independent ; we are at war ; we are victors. The representative of the emperor, his generals and commanders,—of that emperor who numbers us in Europe as his vassals, who marks our country as his own on the map,—has lately opened communication with the Circassians, not to offer pardon for rebellion, but to bargain for the retreat of twenty thousand men, who are surrounded by

our people, and to make arrangements for the exchange of prisoners of war."

Our journey from Vadran to Soutchali, where
we spent a night, occupied the greatest part of
a day; the distance might be about twenty-five
miles. Here we were received by a rich usden,
Adelgerie Achmet, one of the principal chiefs of
the district, who welcomed us with the same hospitality, the same cordiality, with which we were
everywhere uniformly greeted. During our route
we passed the little bay of Mamai, so inconsiderable as not to serve as a harbour for any vessels, save the little skippers of the natives and
the Turks.

At Soutchali, I observed that a decided change
had taken place in the physical aspect of the
people, and even in some of their customs and
manners, differing widely from the inhabitants of
Lower Abasia, or, more properly speaking, of that
part of Circassia between Djook and the Kouban,
which is inhabited principally by Kabardah-Cir-
cassians, that is to say, pure Circassians, who
flocked thither in great numbers, on account of
the province of Kabardah being in the immediate
vicinity of the great military road Wladi-Kaukas,
and also because Kabardah does not offer the

same facilities of defence in elevated mountains
and strong defiles as those provinces of Circassia
immediately on the coast.

We are everywhere reminded of this change by
the light elastic form of the agile and active peasant, by his dark-brown hair, prominent nose,
narrow face, ears like those of the Jews, and a
head more compressed than we usually see among
the Circassians; the latter, in this as in every
other particular of their external physical con-
formation, resembling some of the most favourable
specimens of the European population.

The Circassian knights do not number the
Abasian tribes among their own family, regarding
them as a people who had come under their dominion by conquest. The Abasians call themselves Absné, while in the Russian, Tartar, and
Circassian dialects they are termed Abasa, and
their neighbours, the Georgians, denominate them
Abkasete.

It is supposed, from ancient records and traditions, that the Abasians in an especial manner
belong to the aboriginal tribes of the Caucasus,
and were at one time a powerful people. According to the records of Georgia, they were governed by their own kings, and at a later period

fell under the sway of the sovereigns of Georgia, until the Circassians, having been driven from the low countries on the banks of the Kouban, and the isle of Taman, by the descendants of Ghenghis-Khan, fled to the mountains of Abasia, from whence they expelled the Georgians, and established a species of sovereignty over the natives, which they continue to hold to this day, as nearly the whole of the chiefs and usdens in that province claim common origin with the Circassians, except those who rule over the Tartar tribes, that people still recognising the authority of the descendants of their ancient sultans, agreeably to treaties made with the Circassian knights on the Tartar tribes establishing themselves in the Caucasus. They are, however, obliged to pay the same deference as the other tribes to any Circassian chief who may encamp in their vicinity, and also to furnish their quota of troops in aid of the common cause. It is remarkable that the Abasians, notwithstanding they were long subject to the Georgian kings, and have since been to the Circassians,—notwithstanding that several Circassian and Tartar tribes have resided among them for centuries,—still preserve their individuality, still retain the language of their ancestors, which, like that of the Circassians, does not bear the slightest affinity to any other, either European or Asiatic, now known, not even to the Circassian itself, with the exception of a few words common to both.

Perhaps no characteristic of the Caucasian tribes is more singular than that which I have said distinguishes the Abasians, namely, their individuality. This is no doubt owing to the custom that, with few exceptions, each tribe intermarries only with its own members; hence, whether it be Circassian, Tartar, Abasian, or any other, the individuals of each exhibit a physical resemblance so decided, that we might deem them to be children of the same family.

The remaining tribes inhabiting the Caucasus, the Lesghians, Ingushes, Ossetinians, Karatchai, &c., even the Georgians, among whom we may include the Imeritians and Mingrelians, each speak a separate dialect peculiar to themselves, and differ essentially in their customs and manners.

This want of agreement in the national features of the Caucasian tribes has not only been the means of sowing feuds and dissensions among themselves, but has materially aided Russia in her designs. *Divide and conquer!* has contributed more than the force of arms in enabling that power to establish the precarious sovereignty she now exercises over some of the districts in the Eastern Caucasus ; a sovereignty of which the natives are already impatient, and will indignantly throw off whenever a propitious moment may present itself.

CHAPTER XXI.

Sketch of the early history of the Abasians—Their personal appearance—Extraordinary agility—Manners and customs—Fertility of the soil—Picturesque beauty of the country—Alps—Romantic attachment of mountaineers in general to liberty —Similarity of the Circassians to the Swiss in the day of Tell—Rarity of crime in the Caucasus.

THE Abasians were known to Strabo under their present appellation. He describes them as a predatory people, pirates at sea, and robbers on land,—a character in a great measure applicable to them in the present day, it being a custom established among this people from time immemorial to plunder every stranger who enters the country, except he is provided with testimonials, entitling him to the protection of a chief; and any vessel that may happen to touch their coast fares no better, unless the captain is furnished with a similar species of passport, or can indisputably prove that he belongs to a friendly power.

Among all the Caucasian tribes, none are more fierce, none more hostile to foreign dominion, than the Abasians, for they suffered themselves to be nearly exterminated before they yielded to the Circassian knights. Although in physical force they are undoubtedly inferior to the Herculean structure and stately form of the latter, they are said to surpass them in agility, cunning, stratagem, and treachery towards their foe. Admirable horsemen, swift of foot, they bound from crag to crag, from precipice to precipice, like their own mountain chamois.

Since the subjugation of their neighbours, the Mingrelians, and the encroachments of Russia upon their territories, the border tribes have frequently, when hard pressed, given in their adhesion, with the intention of retracting it on the first favourable opportunity ; and which they never failed to execute, rising *en masse* and murdering her soldiers. Indeed, they are the most inveterate enemies of Russia, and are sworn, like the Circassian knights, their feudal rulers, never to recognise her authority,—a determination which the peculiar nature of their country enables them to carry into effect.

To contend against such a people, inhabiting the strongest defiles in the Caucasus, led on by chiefs whose energetic character renders war a pastime, must appear hopeless, more especially when it is remembered that the whole long line of coast they inhabit on the Black Sea does not contain a single bay or creek that can be deemed a safe harbour for the merchantman, with the exception of Djook, Pitzounda, and Soukoum-Kalé, and even these are not so at every season of the year.

In consequence of the long rule of the Circassian knights over the Abasians, they resemble that people in their dress and many of their domestic habits, and, like them, never leave home without being completely armed.

We find no villages among the Abasians, and their hamlets, instead of being arranged in squares and circles, with a court for their cattle in the interior, like those of the Circassians, stand detached, on the banks of some rivulet or gushing spring, on the side of a mountain.

Their dwellings consist of several cots for themselves, their visitors, and cattle. The exterior and interior exactly resemble those of the Circassians I have already described; and in hospitality and attention to the stranger, of whose truth and fidelity they have received testimonials, the Abasians will bear a comparison with any other of the Caucasian tribes.

It has been erroneously remarked by former writers, that the Abasians are a migratory race, like the Tartars, a remark which has originated in consequence of this people, like other mountaineers, having the custom of leading their cattle to the tops of the high hills during a few months in summer, for the sake of the herbage, where they encamp in tents of felt, resembling those of the Tartars.

Owing to the mountainous character of Abasia, the fields are not extensive; notwithstanding, the poorest peasant has his little farm, consisting of pasturage for his cattle, land for agriculture, and wood for fuel, which he surrounds with a neat paling; hence they appear like so many pretty little domains, and not only add to the picturesque character of the landscape, but impart to the country the aspect of being most abundantly populated.

The arable lands of the Abasians, being usually

situated on the southern declivity of a hill, are extremely fertile, as are also those of their valleys exposed to the rays of the sun ; while the less favoured spots furnish sufficient pasturage for their cattle. Their domestic animals are those common to the Caucasus, and their horses are equal in beauty to any others in these provinces. They have, however, an inferior race of horses, which are employed in carrying burdens and in agricultural pursuits.

As may be supposed, a country like Abasia, possessing a southern aspect to the Euxine, and splendid mountains, covered with rich forests, valleys and defiles, with their brawling streams, added to all the characteristics of alpine scenery, abounds in the most romantic and picturesque prospects.

In one place we see rocks and precipices jutting up from among virgin forests, like so many pyramids, in all their grotesque forms. In another, sloping fields, with their groups of tiny cots ; here rivulets rushing down majestic hills like so many cascades, and there luxuriant meadows and pastures covered with flocks and herds. Again, we have only to ascend any one of its stupendous mountains, when we have on one side the vast expanse of the Euxine spread out before us, and on the other the mighty Elberous and Mkinvari towering in majestic grandeur to the heavens; while at the same time we behold hills of a lesser elevation gradually descending, like gigantic stepping stones, towards the marshes of the Kouban and the plains of Mingrelia.

How anxiously I wished to ascend the co-lossal Elberous, whose stupendous height made it appear as a pillar raised to support the vast arch of heaven, a region never pressed by the foot of a European, from whose seas of eternal ice issue the thousand torrents that fertilize the whole of the Caucasus and the adjacent plains. How desirous was I to explore this magnificent range now spread out before me, whose loftiest sum-mits are some thousand feet higher than the far-famed Mont Blanc!—and what a field is there not here opened to the researches of future travellers! The grandest sublimities of nature, whatever can inspire man, or exalt his imagination,—all that is wild, terrific or romantic,—may here be found; and what can be more calculated to elevate the mind than the contemplation of these stupendous works of the Almighty? A beautiful work of art, a splendid structure, may excite admiration;

but how insignificant are they, compared with the architecture of nature, its precipices, gigantic masses of rock, glaciers, and eternal snow, moulded in all their varied, beautiful, and grotesque forms.

Absorbed in surprised delight, we remember no more the privations, the fatigue, of travelling, and journey onward, unmindful of all else save the grand scenes we are contemplating. Neither must we forget that these alps are situated in a country perhaps the most interesting in our hemisphere, favoured with a climate where glaciers mingle with valleys teeming with all the luxuriant productions and choicest fruits of the south of Europe, where a journey of a few hours suffices to transport the traveller from a heat intense as that which scorches the soil of Arabia, to a cold which might freeze the cheerless waste of Siberia, and which tends to produce an endless variety in the scenery and productions.

At every step some new charm, some new feature, develops itself. Nor are the manners and customs of the inhabitants less interesting than their patriotism, attachment to the ancient usages of their forefathers, and perhaps above all the extraordinary stand they have made, for

the last fifty years, against one of the greatest
empires the earth has witnessed since that of
the Romans, who, if she cannot boast of bound-
less wealth, vast resources, and legions of un-
daunted bravery, more than atones for these de-
ficiencies by a well-regulated army of diploma-
tists, whose manœuvres are directed with a skill
and tact unequalled by those of any other nation. To this we may add, that she possesses
a cabinet highly accomplished in all the arts of
political intrigue, which never fails to advance
her own interests at the expense of her opponents.

But to return to the Circassians, and their
magnanimous struggle against the encroachments
of their formidable neighbour. If the Swiss, in
their most glorious days, repelled successfully the
iron-cased knights of Germany, at the head of their
mercenary but well-disciplined legions, they were
nearly equal to their opponents, at least, in point
of weapons. Whereas here we have a people who,
amidst the roar and blaze of a tremendous force
of artillery, and with no other defensive power
than the rifle and the sword, have hitherto not only
maintained their independence, but, year after
year, are the victors. In short, the deeds of that

band of Swiss patriots immortalized by the names of Tell, Staubach, and Fürst, never shone with more heroic splendour than those of the Caucasian mountaineers,—deeds unknown to civilized Europe, because Russia never publishes a bulletin of her victories or defeats in the Caucasus, and because the triumphs of these mountaineers are never recorded by any other historian, save the simple extemporary effusions of their native bards.

It would appear as if the unconquerable passion for liberty were congenial to the mountaineer of every country, as if the very aspect of his own stupendous hills and gloomy fastnesses imparted to him a spirit of freedom, gave boldness and intrepidity to his efforts in its cause, and armed him with a strength sufficient to trample down tyranny and tyrants, however powerful. We have seen in our own day the Tyrolean peasant crush the choicest legions of Europe's greatest captain, and we now behold a handful of Basque mountaineers holding in check, and defying, millions of their lowland brethren: may we not then be assured that, if the Caucasian tribes, notwithstanding their different dialects and forms of government, continue to maintain that concord and union so happily established

among them by the efforts of a friendly stranger,
they must finally triumph, and those valleys that
are now polluted by the ravages of a licentious
soldiery become, like Switzerland, at no very distant period, the magnet of attraction to all the
tourists of Europe? for her scenery is not more
romantic, the rare plants and herbs that flower
on her mountains are not more interesting to the
botanist, nor her mines to the mineralogist, while
the traveller will have the advantage of exploring
a country in which the people are more simple
in their manners, more pastoral in their pursuits,
and by far more courteous and hospitable to the
stranger : and what a field will there not be laid
open to the curious, and those interested in the
history of nations, in the study of the store of
legendary ballads and traditions of perhaps the
most interesting people of every other to a European.

It may appear incredible to some of my readers,
but murder, robbery, or even petty thefts, are
nearly unknown among the allied tribes of the
Caucasus in their dealings with each other; and
this notwithstanding there is neither police,
house of correction, or any other check upon
their evil inclinations than the stern reproof of

their patriarchs, and the dread of fine and banishment. However lightly they may regard honesty
in their dealings with the stranger of whose good
intentions they have no warrant,—however merciless they may be in pursuit of an enemy,—kindness, hospitality, and all the charities of social
life, characterize their conduct to each other.
By these humane sentiments, and many other
observances, particularly the possession, by the
inhabitants of many hamlets, of property in common, the equitable division of their profits and
the fruits of their predatory incursions, war, &c.,
they lose the semblance of savage life, and are
far more happy than the rapacious European, who
is never contented when wealth is the object to be
acquired.

Strangers to the vices of civilized life, inordi-
nate luxury, sordid selfishness, and love of gain,
their ancient simplicity of manners remains un-
corrupted, which renders them so much more
interesting to a European. The same detestation
of effeminate indulgences, the same blunt honesty,
love of truth, and affection for the land of their
fathers—characteristics which won for the ancient
Swiss their liberty—are those which now distinguish the allied tribes of the Western Caucasus.

Indeed, this regard for truth, and horror of treachery in friendly intercourse, is so great, that, although they hesitate at no evasion, no falsehood, no crime, in their dealings with an enemy, the man that would betray his friend, or has recourse to deception to gain his point, is despised by his compatriots, and treated with as much contempt as if he had deserted his comrades on the field of battle—in their opinion, by the bye, the greatest of all crimes.

CHAPTER XXII.

Religion of the Abasians—Their sacred groves—Superstitious veneration for springs—Ceremonies performed before going to battle—Duels—Throwing the djerrid.

THE religion of the Abasians, like that of nearly the whole of the Caucasians, is a compound of Judaism, Christianity, and Islamism : they worship only one God, as the giver of all good, and the creator of the universe. Certain saints, for the sake of their supposed power as mediators between mortals and the Divinity, are highly reverenced ; but by whom this power was delegated they acknowledge themselves entirely ignorant, having received the tradition from their ancestors. We may, however, I think, regard it as a relic of catholicism.

To the Saviour and his divine attributes they are utter strangers, while they are familiar with the character of Moses as a lawgiver, and Elijah as a prophet, who ascended to heaven in a chariot of fire; and, singular to say, most of the Caucasian tribes celebrate the Lord's day (Sunday) in preference to the Jewish or Mahometan sabbath, as a day of rest from labour. In spring, they observe a fast of seven, and in summer, one of nine, weeks; and, like the Jews, keep the feast of the Passover: their marriages, burials, births, &c., are attended with nearly the same ceremonies as the Mahometans. Still they do not obey the injunction of Mahomet, to abstain from eating swine's flesh, that of the wild boar being highly esteemed; nay, some of the tribes even go the length of keeping herds of these unclean animals, probably more for the purposes of barter with the Cossacks and the Christians of Mingrelia and Imeritia than for their own consumption,—always taking care, however, to play the part of good Mahometans before a stranger whom they consider as a devotee of that faith. Indeed, most of the Circassian princes and nobles inhabiting the coast profess the tenets of Islamism, so far, at least, as regards its external observances, and even maintain a moullah about their household, who occasionally chants a few passages from the Koran, in

Arabic, not one word of which do either he or his flock understand !

Some writers pretend, judging from the architecture of the ruins of ancient convents and churches found in Abasia, and which correspond with those erected by the famous Georgian Queen Thamar, in her own dominions, that she originally introduced among the Caucasians the Christian religion, about the early part of the twelfth century.

These ruins are still regarded with great veneration by the natives, and, as sanctuaries for the criminal, inviolably respected. They are also the object of pilgrimages to those devotees who would implore some especial favour from the Divinity, or expiate a crime.

The Abasians also resemble the Circassians in their attachment to sacred groves, in which every warrior belonging to the district of any particular grove appropriates to himself a tree, which he adorns with some trophy of his victories, and likewise with offerings indicative of his gratitude to the Divinity for blessings received. Before they go forth to battle, the whole of the warriors are accustomed to assemble in these sacred groves, when the oldest, wisest, and bravest patriarch

among them takes a sword, and, striking an
aged oak, exhorts his young companions to
deeds of bravery; and, mentioning the name or
the enemy they are about to combat, urges them
to kill, slay, and destroy without mercy, or submit to see their fields taken away from them,
their women captives, and they themselves led
in chains. Then, addressing the oak, he continues—" Sacred tree, thou hast witnessed, from
time immemorial, the performance of this ceremony by our fathers! They have conquered!
may their blessed spirits hover over us, their
children, and guide our swords to victory!"

If the attack is directed against the Russians,
he concludes by saying—" Remember, the man
that falls in this contest is immediately translated
to paradise." This belief of a happy immortality,
when they die fighting against Russia, being universal among the Caucasian tribes.

To cut down a tree in these sacred groves, or
to despoil them of their offerings, is considered
sacrilege—a crime of the deepest dye, and which
it is lawful for the person robbed to punish with
death. Several of these sacred groves, in the
vicinity of the coast, have been from time to
time cut down by the Russian armies, during

their progress through the country, no doubt for the purpose of facilitating the passage of the troops, and also to destroy a covert from which the mountaineers could safely direct their attacks.

The Circassians, however, behold the act in a very different point of view, considering it as one of wanton sacrilege, and which of course tends to increase tenfold the animosity of a superstitious people against their invaders, whom they brand as profane infidels, among the other epithets of contempt which they bestow on that nation.

Besides these sacred groves, certain springs, in secluded romantic situations, are also highly venerated, for of these crystal streams their fathers drank, and watered their flocks and herds. Consequently, the man who violates their sanctity by polluting them, or cutting down a tree in their vicinity, incurs the guilt of sacrilege; for, say the mountaineers, " our fathers, on arriving from the parched desert, found friendly shelter beneath their venerable shade."

We have said that the mountaineers of Abasia are inferior to the Circassians in personal appearance; still, they are a fine race of men, and would be considered handsome in any country. Their features exhibit a mingled expression of

fierce independence and seriousness. Though
they cannot be termed stout men, and never exceed the middle size, their physical structure indicates strength and activity.

The sterner passions of our nature they display without any attempt at restraint; but though
violent in temper when irritated, they are soon
pacified when reproved by their patriarchs. On
the most trifling provocation, a fiery youth, un-
chastened by the trials of life, seizes his sabre,
but never uses fire-arms against one of his own
tribe, nor an ally, these weapons being reserved
to avenge the blood of a friend, or to repel the invaders of their land.

A stranger, on witnessing for the first time one
of these duelling combats—which, by the way,
are not unfrequent among a people so sensitive
to an insult—would conclude, from the violence
of the encounter, that one of the combatants
must inevitably fall. No such thing; for each
parries the attack of the other with so much
adroitness, that at length they retire from the
contest utterly exhausted with fatigue, and generally without receiving so much as a single
scratch.

These encounters being usually fought on

horseback, no European can form the most distant conception of their agility, and the extraordinary address they display in avoiding the deadly
blows of each other, dealt with a fierceness and
a strength sufficient to hew down an ox. But
this is not all; their immovable firmness in the
saddle, the simultaneous motion of the horse and
his rider, might well have originated the fable of
the centaur. During these terrific encounters,
their comrades look on with as much *sang-froid*
as if they were beholding a game of shuttle-cock.

But of all the exhibitions I witnessed among
the Circassian warriors, that of throwing the
djerrid afforded me the greatest pleasure; this
being one of the favourite amusements pursued
in the camps. For this purpose, a certain number of combatants assemble, belonging probably
to two different districts, each mounted on a
magnificent steed, and armed with a long white
stave.

At a signal given by their respective chiefs,
they all set off at full gallop in pursuit of each
other, when staves are seen flying about in every
direction. However, the most interesting and
surprising part of the scene is, the dexterity with
which they contrive to elude each other's blow,

catch a stave, or pick up one which may be dropped, without alighting, or losing a moment's time. Here, a horseman who happens to be without a djerrid, or has become entangled among his opponent's party, may be seen twisting and turning, with all the activity of a wild cat, in order to elude the blow aimed at him, and save himself from the disgrace of a broken head: now completely screened under the belly of his horse, then lying in full length on its back, and again stretched on the side, until he regains a djerrid, and becomes, in his turn, the assailant.

To a European it appears almost impossible that the human body could be capable of assuming so many different attitudes; but what will not persevering practice effect? Indeed, it is principally owing to these athletic games—and no doubt that the climate acts materially upon the frame—that the Circassians excel every other people in equestrian and such warlike exercises as require quickness in action and agility.

CHAPTER XXIII.

Domestic manners of the Abasians—Industry of the women —Abasian armourers—Excellence of their weapons— Circassian knights—Their pride of birth—Laws of the Abasians respecting illegitimate children—The distribution of property—Enforcement of morality—Divorce— Filial obedience.

POLYGAMY, according to the ancient laws and customs of the Abasians, is permitted; but as a wife, in the Caucasus, cannot be obtained but by purchase, it may be for this reason that they are usually contented with one. Contrary to the practice of the Islamites, a wife is more the companion than the menial of her husband. While the wives and daughters of the Circassian knights, who are more Turkish in their manners, reside in separate habitations from their lords, and are only visible to the hakkim or distinguished guest, the peasant dwells in the same cot with his wife and family, and does not seclude them from social intercourse with their neighbours or strangers.

The same laws, observances, and ceremonies as those of the Circassians, with regard to marriages, divorce, education of children, &c., are observed by the Abasians.

The women are extremely industrious: during the time their husbands are engaged in war, the chace, and warlike exercises, they employ themselves not only in domestic affairs, but in manufacturing cloth, making clothes for their families, attending to their flocks and herds,—even in agricultural pursuits. They are generally handsome, particularly the young, who, glowing with the rosy hue of health, imparted to them from the bracing air of the mountains, are sprightly, naïve, and interesting. Their style of wearing the hair and head-dress resembles those of the Circassian women, which is very becoming; and, like them, they are fully sensible of the advantages of a pretty person and a fine complexion, for the better classes never go out of doors without gloves on their hands, a thick veil to screen themselves from the beams of the sun, and in wet weather high clogs to preserve themselves from the ill effects of the damp; indeed, the Caucasians of

both sexes must be extremely poor if they are
seen without a covering for the feet.

Both men and women are extremely fond of
ornamental dresses. Those of the former are
adorned with borders of silver embroidery, neatly
executed, the work of the women. The silver
and gold arabesque-work on their belts and weapons is done with a skill and ingenuity surprising
to a European, when he compares their secluded
situation and simple mode of living with so much
ingenious talent as artificers. I doubt if the temper of their weapons can be equalled in Europe.
The Circassian knights, who are good judges,
generally procure their swords and poniards from
the Abasians, who are eminently skilful as
armourers. Whether this superiority arises from
the nature of the Caucasian metal, or the peculiar
excellence of the method of preparing it, I was
unable to ascertain, as the tribes who manufacture these weapons live at some distance from the
coast.

The women, on their part, decorate their robes,
which resemble those of the Circassians, with
broad borders of coloured embroidery, and complete their dress with a large veil, either white or
some gay colour; the effect of the whole is

showy, and not unbecoming.   The colour of the
trowsers indicates whether the wearer be maid,
wife, or widow,—virgin-white being worn by the
young girl, red by her who has assumed the
duties of the matron, and blue by the hapless, or,
it may be, the happy dame who has survived her
lord.

As these tribes, to which we may add the whole
of the Caucasians, are extremely partial to dress,
I must be of the opinion that a cargo of bright-
coloured woollen, silk, or cotton stuffs, would be
received with avidity, and ensure an enormous
profit, in the way of exchange, to the merchant ;
as would also a supply of pistols, and gun-barrels,
with the locks, the Caucasians preferring their
own method of mounting fire-arms.

The chiefs and nobles of Abasian origin do not
rank so high as the aristocratic Circassian, who
assumes, in this respect, a superiority not only
over every other tribe in the Caucasus, but those
of the surrounding nations, maintaining that no
family can be noble that ever intermarried with
those of inferior degree.   Indeed, there are no
people who value themselves on the pride of high
birth more than the princes of Circassia ; consequently, few instances occur of unequal mar-

riages, the son of a prince invariably taking for his wife the daughter of a prince, and a noble the daughter of one of his own rank ; but a Circassian noble is always equal in rank, according to their customs and laws, to a prince of any other tribe, nation, or country.

The opinion entertained in Europe, that the princes and nobles of Circassian origin sell their daughters, without regard to rank, to the Turks and Persians, for their seraglios, is incorrect. The usual mode, I was informed, when the fame of the beauty of some Circassian princess has reached the ears of any oriental prince or sovereign, is, to open a negociation with her father for the hand of his fair daughter, and, after the treaty has been brought to a successful conclusion, he receives, according to eastern usage, in exchange for his daughter, handsome and adequate presents. Most of the girls sold in the bazaars of Constantinople and the principal towns of Asia Minor and Persia, as Circassians, are either Abasians, or the children of Circassian peasants, or captives taken from the neighbouring Cossacks, or from those Caucasian tribes who have given in their adhesion to Russia.

The Abasians, like the Circassians, consider contempt of life as a virtue, and, sooner than submit to slavery, or pine under misfortune and degradation, destroy themselves. This feeling is not more prevalent among the men than the women, who frequently, sooner than become the captives of their enemies, rush wildly upon the point of their weapons. Several instances of this were related to me by the Ataman of the Tchernemorsky Cossacks whom I met while travelling in Krim-Tartary.

The fate of illegitimate children would be deplorable in the Caucasus, were it not for the kindness inherent in these people, for, according to the laws and customs of nearly the whole of the Caucasian tribes, they have not only no claim upon the patrimonial inheritance, but are totally unconnected with any person by the ties of consanguinity; consequently, should they be sold as slaves, there is no friendly hand to ransom them, or die by the hand of an assassin, no relative to avenge the deed; and they are even liable to be put to death by their legitimate brothers. Still, it rarely happens that they are treated with harshness; and their legitimate brethren, out of respect to the memory of their father, often share with them the property he has left, and protect them through life.

On the other hand, should a Caucasian have no issue by his wife, he takes to himself her handmaid, like Abraham, whose children succeed their father in all his possessions and privileges, as if they were his legitimate offspring.

In the same manner, the illegitimate son of a Circassian prince or noble cannot succeed to any portion of the property of his father, nor his titles, unless his bravery, eloquence, and abilities, win for him the esteem of his legitimate brethren, who generally bestow upon him, by way of courtesy, the title of their father, and treat him in every respect as a brother; but even should he attain the hand of a princess, the ignominy still pursues his offspring, who cannot hold any title beyond that of a second-rate noble.

When a man dies, let his rank be what it may, custom gives to his wife the superintendence of the domestic department, and she continues to administer the property, without division, till her death, when each son takes his share, or they join together, and form one common interest; the greatest share, however, descending, by right of birth, to the firstborn. Should any of the sisters happen to be unmarried, they become subject to their eldest brother, and form part of his inheritance, he being bound to provide for them till he can dispose of them advantageously in marriage; and when his fair wards are young and pretty, they become the sources to him of no inconsiderable number of flocks and herds; but no time must be lost in finding them husbands, for a Circassian woman, after eighteen, becomes very much depreciated in value.

The laws against immorality are extremely severe. If a man is detected in carrying on an illicit intercourse with either a married or unmarried woman, he is tried before the elders of his tribe, who rarely fail to punish him, according to the circumstances under which the offence had been committed, with a heavy fine, or perpetual banishment. The dishonoured wife, after being returned to her parents, is sold as a slave, and a single woman shares the same fate. The dowry, also, which the husband had given for her, is returned to him. But should it happen to be the wife or daughter of a prince who has thus disgraced her family, the stain can only be washed out with the blood of the paramour, and I believe, in most instances, with that of the woman. So poignantly, indeed, is this dishonour felt, that a family on whom it has been inflicted usually retire to a remote part of the Caucasus, there to conceal the shame which has degraded them in public estimation for ever.

Divorce is not unfrequent. When this is the case, the husband is obliged to declare, in the presence of the elders, his reasons for the separation; and should these not be found perfectly satisfactory, he must give a sufficient recompence to the father for the burden thus thrown upon him. Should the lady contract a second marriage before the expiration of two years, the recompence is returned to her first husband. It not unfrequently happens, as in other countries, that a girl strongly dislikes the husband selected for her by her father, or forms a romantic attachment to some youth of her connexions; in such cases she has been known to fly to the woods, and there remain for months, a fugitive from the parental roof, rather than yield herself a bride to the man she detests.

Again, it sometimes happens that two different warriors are captivated by the charms of the same beauty. In this case, instead of having recourse to the amicable expedient, "the highest bidder shall be the buyer," they resort to a duel; and such is the animosity with which the rivals regard each other, that they have been known to go so far as to fight with the last resource, fire-arms. The victor, of course, becomes the husband of the lady.

If a son is disobedient to his parents, or if his conduct should be so flagrantly bad as to cause him to be publicly admonished by the elders, and if, notwithstanding their reproof, he perseveres in his course of disobedience to his father and to the laws, he draws down upon himself the curse of his parent, when, from that awful moment, he becomes an outcast from society—a wretch to be shunned by all, branded, like Cain, with the mark which proclaims him to be a man who has deserved the opprobrium of the whole human race.

These, and many others, are the patriarchal laws of this singular and romantic people, for the preservation of morality and the punishment of vice,—laws and customs peculiarly well adapted to a people so primitive in their habits, so remote from the temptations of civilized life, from its wants, comforts, and all its train of evils; and those who have witnessed the manner in which they float down the stream of life, may well say, with the philosopher, " Man wants but little here below ;" and the less he wants, the greater is his happiness.

In this patriarchal land we find no splendid equipages, no fine houses, with their costly furniture and liveried lacqueys, no object to create envy or excite a desire in the Circassian to obtain the possessions of his neighbour ; for, with the exception of nominal rank and title, there is scarce a shade of difference between the condition of the peasant and his prince ; birth, virtue, and valour, being the only distinctions in Circassia. And as to their patriarchal customs, not all the restraining laws ever invented by the ingenuity of man could have greater efficacy in deterring the youth of this country from evil than the dread of a parent's malediction ; hence it is seldom provoked.

In consequence of this dread of a father's curse, we behold examples of filial duty and obedience in these people, denounced to us by their enemies as barbarians, which might cause a blush in the well-instructed disciples of Christianity. Here no parent ever wanders from door to door to seek from the cold hand of a stranger that

bread which is denied him by a child, living perhaps in luxury, and who now, elevated by fickle
fortune to wealth, is ashamed to own affinity with
the wretched, helpless being who claims to be his
parent.

Did we give credit to the traducers of this
people (the Caucasian tribes in general), who re-
present them as hordes of vagabonds, lawless
depredators, without a government or a law, every
man's sword turned against his brother, idolators
in worship, and immoral in their conduct,—a
people that no kindness can tame, so treacherous
that no treaties can bind, and who will not hesitate to slay with one hand while the other tenders
the bread of hospitality,—we should rejoice at
the prospect of their being brought beneath the
government of some civilized power, however
much it might tend to disturb the equilibrium of
nations.

But how different is their real character, which
I have drawn according to the dictates of truth,
without being influenced either by partiality or
sympathy for their condition, and for the accuracy of which I relied not only on my own observations, but on the representations of those
who had lived long among them.   Besides, I

would ask the impartial observer of the tendencies of human nature, how is it possible that any people could exist so utterly barbarous as they are said to be,—a race of lawless, sanguinary banditti? Why, half a century would, owing to the mutual wars they are reported to carry on, have sufficed to render the most fertile, the most populous country in the universe, a desert.

CHAPTER XXIV.

OUR day's ride along the beach between Soutchali and Ardler was long and fatiguing, having
occupied us full twelve hours, including an hour's
rest at noon, and may be from about thirty-five
to forty miles. When we take into consideration
the nature of the ground over which we travelled,
composed for the most part of pebbles and sand
from the sea, with here and there a rugged hill
to cross, we cannot deem it a bad day's journey

for a horse. A minute description of the scenery would only be a repetition of what I have already given. The landscape was, however, more diversified, presenting, in addition to the usual features of verdant mountains, meandering rivulets, fertile valleys, and the majestic expanse of the Euxine, a more distinctly defined prospect of the snow-clad alps at whose base we had now for some time journeyed, as this great chain commences at the defile of Jagra, immediately on the coast, in a majestic mountain of porphyry, flanked with limestone rocks. The other range, extending to Anapa, in mountain plateaus of decreasing elevation, is not considered by Russian geologists as forming a part of the Elberous chain, for what reason I am unable to determine, it being, in fact, if I may so speak, the basement story of the same mighty structure, presenting, as they do, the same combination of primitive, volcanic, and limestone rocks, with here and there a ridge of porphyry, slate, or granite.

We were disappointed in our hope of finding a vessel at the little bay of Ardler, to convey us to the Turkish coast; for such had been the violence of the late storm, that not one of the many little Turkish trading vessels that visit the coast of

Circassia had yet made their appearance : nor did
we, during the whole of our route, perceive a
single Russian man-of-war ; they were, no doubt,
still lying snugly at anchor in some quiet tempest-
screened nook.

We were, however, not disappointed in finding
a friend at Ardler, in the chief of the district, who
conducted us to his house, situated about two
miles up the country, and treated us with true
Circassian hospitality.   Here we also met with
several other chiefs and usdens of the neighbouring tribes, together with Kurtschock Ali, the
cousin of my young friend Beisroukou, the son
of one of the chiefs of the Barrakai, a warlike
tribe, situated in that part of the snowy mountains where the Chotz, the Laba, and their tributary streams have their source; the district is called
by the Circassians, Shikilbuluku, and is about two
days' journey, through the interior, from Ardler.
His father is said to be one of the bravest knights,
and determined enemies of Russia, in the Caucasus ; and, if we might judge from the appearance
of the son, he is likely to have a worthy successor.
He was, in truth, a fine, noble-looking fellow,
with an eye like that of one of his own alpine
eagles, and, being habited like the other Abasian

chiefs, in complete armour, (a general custom in the Caucasus when distinguished guests are entertained) presented a martial bearing that might have served for one of Rome's proud warriors in the days of her greatest triumphs.

As our host resides in the vicinity of the Russian fortresses, Pitzounda, Bombora, and Soukoum-Kalé, he and his tribe, with their allies, the Kubichan, Kâsilbeg, the Besliné, Besubbeh, &c., have little time for repose, being continually occupied in repelling the sorties of the garrisons in their search after provisions, forage, and water. He amused his brother knights by relating the details of his various encounters with the enemy, and the snares by which he had succeeded in luring them into his power, and seemed to regard their vicinity with the same cool determination as an experienced hunter would a lion at bay, the rocky dells of his country at all times securing to him and his tribe a safe retreat from any serious attack, while they form a bulwark from which they can conveniently take murderous aim, without being in any danger themselves.

He had thrown up intrenchments round the little village in which he resided with his dependents, and defended them with a couple of brass guns taken from the Russians, and a few iron howitzers made by himself, of which contrivance he was not a little proud. In addition to this, he had also fortified several of the narrow passes with stone walls; but powder—powder—was the great desideratum.

Since the more rigid enforcement of the blockade, the Circassians have begun to purchase this article from the Karatchai, or, as the Circassian knights call them, Karshaga-Kusha (Black Tartars), whose mountains produce abundance of sulphur and saltpetre: their powder is excellent, and strong, but, owing to the difficulty of transporting it across the snowy mountains, the Circassian warriors prefer, except when there is an urgent necessity for an immediate supply, to procure it from the Turks in exchange for their own productions.

Man is the same every where; and any interruption in the usual routine of affairs is at first sensibly felt, until absolute necessity compels him to fabricate the article he requires, or some efficient substitute. In process of time, no doubt, the mountaineers of the Caucasus will manufacture sufficient gunpowder for themselves, without relying on the

Turks for a supply, as the country abounds with the materials for making it ; and as to salt, beside the long line of coast they have on the Euxine still in their possession, I pointed out to my Circassian friends several salt springs, during my excursion, which might, if properly managed, furnish sufficient to meet the wants of the tribes in the vicinity, instead of which they are accustomed to season their food with skhou (a species of sour milk), as a substitute ; and, singular to say, although many tribes in the interior rarely ever touch salt, by using the skhou, their health, as I before observed, is not in the slightest degree deranged. But a people like the Circassians, so passionately attached to their equestrian exercises, war, and hunting, and, in time of repose, to agriculture, tending their flocks and herds, and domestic arrangements,—for they are all, prince and peasant, their own carpenters, builders, and upholsterers,—find little leisure to occupy themselves as manufacturers and artificers, occupations always considered by the Circassian knight as derogatory to his dignity. Still they are shrewd, active, and intelligent ; any hint or suggestion offered to them by a person better instructed than themselves is generally acted upon ; hence their gradual improvement in the arts of civilized life may, with every probability, be predicted.

At Ardler we found several Poles and Russians, who had deserted from the garrisons only a few days previous. They appeared to be well contented with their new friends ; but the natives, on the contrary, did not evince an equal degree of cordiality, fearing that a wolf in sheep's clothing might be lurking among them, and to guard against any such danger, the chief was preparing to send them, under a strong escort, to his brother knights in the interior of the country.

These deserters are usually employed in agricultural pursuits, or as artificers, until they have, by marriage with the natives, acquired the rights of freemen ; or, by their continued good conduct, established themselves in the confidence of the Circassian knights ; or obtained the countenance of some chief or native who will be a guarantee for their fidelity ; they are then allowed to take a part in the more honourable occupation of war.

These people are, as I before observed, extremely jealous of foreigners—resulting partly from a disposition naturally suspicious, and partly from the circumstance that they have been repeatedly deceived by pretended deserters, who, after making themselves acquainted with the fastnesses of the country, with the force and capabilities of defence possessed by the mountaineers, have returned to their comrades ; and the information they have acquired, being acted upon by the Russians, has frequently been productive of fatal consequences to the too confiding natives.

The want of confidence thus generated is the more to be regretted, as the majority of the deserters are men of some talent, refractory Poles, forced to serve in the Russian ranks, or natives of Russia, who, having been found guilty of entertaining political opinions not approved by the government, were drafted into the army of the Caucasus, a species of transportation ; and, as may naturally be expected under these circumstances, they became the most deadly enemies of Russia. It is somewhat singular that, out of the number of Poles now wandering, without a country, without a home, in England, France, and elsewhere,—subsisting upon the miserable pittance wrung from the generosity of foreigners, many being, at the same time, men of distinguished talent and bravery, that not one of eminence has yet found his way to the Caucasus, a *pied-de-terre* pre-eminently calculated for them to carry on operations against their ancient, their implacable foe.

Were only a small number of these men to journey thither, and add their knowledge, experience, and military tactics to the bravery of the people, they might, in a few years, carry fire and sword into the very heart of Russia, weaken the resources of the government, and probably succeed eventually in emancipating their own country. To this we may add there is little doubt, if once victorious, they would find allies in the Cossacks of the Don and Kouban, many of whom claim common origin with the Poles ; and events have shewn of late years that they are wavering in their allegiance.

Besides, no difficulty whatever exists in obtaining recommendatory letters from the friends of Circassia in Constantinople, and even nearer home, to some of the chiefs ; and the danger of getting there, if they act only with common prudence, is a mere scarecrow, for in fine weather, and with a fair wind, the little Turkish vessels have been known to run over from Trebizond, or from any of the ports in Lazestahn, to Upper Abasia, in less than twenty-four hours, in defiance of the Russian blockade.

Neither is there the slightest apprehension to be entertained in an inland excursion across the Turkish frontier, through Gourial and Mingrelia, to Circassia, this being the usual route of the Armenian pedlers and other travellers to Circassia, in winter, or when high winds prevent vessels approaching the coast, — the Russian frontier in that quarter being very indifferently guarded, even during the prevalence of the plague; this results from there being in fact nothing to guard, and no troops to spare from the theatre of war in the Caucasus. In addition to this, there is hardly any communication between the impoverished Lazi on the Turkish side, and the not less miserable Gourials on the Russian side; and the very idea of a hostile attack, at present, from the armies of Turkey's enfeebled monarch, against his generous ally and protector is indeed a chimera. However, such a journey should be undertaken late in the autumn, or during the winter, to ensure complete success, and always in company with a Karaite Jew, or an Armenian pedler, a class of persons who are allowed great liberty and indulgence in their wanderings through the Russian dominions; they must not, however, be trusted too far, as they are

completely and entirely mercenary; these people
generally speak three or four languages, are
quick-witted and shrewd, but artful, inquisitive,
and intriguing.

In consequence of the commercial transactions
of these people with the inhabitants of the Caucasus, they are personally acquainted with most
of the influential chiefs of the different tribes,
and, what is equally important in a guide, are as
familiar with the passes and secret routes; and
whether it arises from fear of losing the very lucrative commerce which they carry on with these people, or from that of losing their heads, I know not,
but it is said that they never betray a Circassian, a
sort of free-masonry appearing in this respect to
be established among them; while the mountaineer,
on his part, always welcomes the man with the
pack, who not only brings him pretty baubles for
his wife and daughters, but a great deal of chit-
chat about proud Stamboul, the city of cities, the
abode of all that is magnificent, splendid, and
wealthy, in his imagination.

The security of travelling through the interior
of Mingrelia, Imeritia, and Gourial, results from
the authority of Russia in these provinces being
extremely limited,—that power, well knowing that

any infringement upon the liberties of a people so tenacious of their freedom, and so easily excited to rebellion, as her subjects in these newly-acquired provinces, might hazard the loss of her authority, which undoubtedly these warlike hordes would endeavour to throw off upon the slightest provocation. Russia, therefore, as a good politician, proceeds cautiously, and has not yet attempted to enforce with strictness her complicated machinery of passports, fiscal laws, quarantine regulations, &c. Neither has she inundated the country with an army of civil employées. In consequence of this, a man recommended to the chiefs may travel over the whole of Imeritia, Mingrelia, and Gourial, if he is accompanied with a native for his guide, at far less risk than if he were guarded by a Russian escort, provided he refrains from visiting the villages in the vicinity of fortified places.

The garrisons even of these are very cautious of irritating the people by intercepting travellers, detaining them as prisoners on suspicion, &c., acts of this description having already led to sanguinary contests with the natives.

When the mountaineers of the Caucasus are subdued, should that event ever take place, there can be no doubt that an entire change in the system of government now pursued in these provinces will take place : then we shall see, as exemplified in the Crimea, and in others of her newly-acquired possessions, the mild paternal rule of the patriarchs and elders superseded by tyranny and despotism, the feudal rights now enjoyed by the chiefs abrogated, the privileges of the people torn from them, and themselves resigned to the merciless exactions of an executive composed of needy adventurers, whose only object being wealth and power, the moral energy of the people will be destroyed in a few years.

Indeed, these beautiful and fertile provinces, situated as they now are, at the very threshold of the theatre of war, inhabited by a population wavering between their allegiance to Russia the determination of joining the mountaineers, are not of the slightest value to that power ; on the contrary, they are not only unproductive, but a constant drain upon her treasury in maintaining a large standing army, and in securing the allegiance of the various influential chiefs and elders by costly gifts presented to them annually, which they in their simplicity regard as a perpetual tribute !

In addition to the disadvantage against which Russia has to contend of ruling over a people alien to her in their customs, manners, and language,—their chiefs, princes, and elders being principally of Circassian origin, and in full possession of their feudal rights, a rebellion in Mingrelia, or in any of the other provinces in the east of the Caucasus, would annihilate her authority in the whole. The tribes residing in the elevated parts of the provinces of Georgia, Imeritia, and Mingrelia,—the Gudamaquaré, the Kewserethi, Pschawi, Tushi, Mithuethi, and many other of Kist and Ossetinian origin, have never been subdued, and still harass the Russian armies in the narrow passes and unfrequented roads leading to these provinces.

These tribes, termed by the Russian government banditti, are said to be bound by an oath, transmitted from father to son, never to submit to the sway of the systematic enemy of the east. This much is certain, no traveller bearing the name of Russian, or who carries a passport from that government, can dare to venture through the country, unless protected by a powerful escort; for, notwithstanding these districts are by no means so strong in defiles and dangerous passes

as the Western Caucasus, still they are everywhere thickly wooded, and abound with craggy
rocks, caverns, and glens,—so that a single band
of marauders, well supplied with ammunition,
might destroy half an army before the other
could discover the lurking places of the enemy.

On the destruction of the Janissaries, and
after the cessation of the civil wars in Persia,
many of the outlawed fugitives here found a
shelter.   These men, together with those discontented with the Russian government in Georgia,
and the other eastern provinces of the Caucasus,
who have joined them, have of late years aggra-
vated the animosity of the people ; and a Russian officer informed me, when in Redout-Kalé,
that they do not scruple to murder his countrymen
for no other cause than being Russian.   He also
added, that as the whole of the Caucasian tribes
are impatient to render themselves independent,
and to establish the government of their own
princes, with their national laws, he much doubted,
after many years of painful experience, whether
any power, however strong and energetic her
measures might be, could succeed in effectually
reducing them, nearly every tribe in the Eastern
Caucasus having repeatedly given in their adhe-

sion to the Russian government, received costly presents and other marks of favour, yet, when a favourable opportunity offered, never failed to revolt and massacre the troops. The Lesghi alone have been at war with Russia for upwards of a century.

CHAPTER XXV.

Departure from Ardler — Accession to our party — Alpine
character of the country—Journey inland—Mingrelians,
their friendship for the Circassians—Abasian rivers—
Valley of the Phandra—A Circassian bride—Bridal cor-
tege—Costume and appointments—Courteous behaviour
of the young Barrakai chief—A scene of chivalry.

On leaving Ardler, we received an addition to
our band in the person of Kurtschock-Ali, the
young Barrakai chief, and his escort, who, after
having made a detour to visit his allies, was now
on his way, in compliance with the custom of the
country, to meet a Karatchai princess, the affi-
anced bride of his brother.

The mountains now rose to a considerable altitude, snow covered the pinnacles of some, while
vast forests extended down their sides, dipping
each feathery branch in the rivulet which laved
their base. The aspect of the country also changed,

becoming more stern in its character, and exhibiting little appearance of population.

We continued our course along the beach till we came to the little river, the Kotoch, when, following its rugged banks, we journeyed towards the interior, and passed the night with one of the chiefs of the Bessubbeh tribe, whose possessions extend to Soukoum-Kalé. This road was taken partly to avoid encountering any of the Russian garrisons at Pitzounda, Bombora, and Soukoum-Kalé, forts which give to Russia the complete mastery over this part of the coast, and partly because it was the nearest route to Imeritia and Georgia, the destination of the chiefs forming our escort, who had also decided on the expediency of our avoiding the coast of Mingrelia, and of penetrating to the centre of the province. At all events, by adopting this route we were certain of being hospitably entertained by the natives; and although they have hitherto, as well as the Imeritians, remained neutral in the quarrel between the mountaineers and Russia, deeply commiserate the fate of the brave Circassians, and aid them in their struggle by supplying them with munitions of war, and salt for their cattle. For these

good offices the grateful mountaineers have re-
frained from carrying the desolation of war into
the plains of Mingrelia, than which nothing could
be more easy, possessing, as they do, the whole
of the mountains which command the province.

After having penetrated about seven or eight
miles into the interior, we left the banks of the Kotoch, and, taking a south-easterly direction, passed
through a deep chasm in the hills, evidently the
bed of some dried-up torrent, being covered with
loose round stones ; this led across a stupendous
ridge to the valley of the Phandra, watered by a
small river of the same name.

Owing to the contiguity of the snowy mountains to the Black Sea in this part of Abasia, not
one of its rivers are navigable, even for the
smallest vessels, being mere rivulets in fine weather, and rushing torrents during the prevalence
of rain ; they are, however, highly valuable to the
mountaineer, their banks affording pasturage
and meadows, and their waters drink, for their
cattle, during the great heats of summer.

Here we met the Karatchai princess, with her
cavalcade of knights and fair dames, her attendants, forming a band altogether of about twenty

persons, the whole of whom were on horseback, and of course well armed,—even the women carried in their belts pistols and poniards.

The princess and her principal women were dressed in scarlet mantles, trimmed with gold lace, and large hats, turned up in front with bands of gold lace and buttons, and ornamented here and there with gold coins. The mantles were stamped with the mark of venerable antiquity in the variety of shades,—in one place faded, in another mended with pieces of a brighter colour; they had probably been heir-looms in the family for centuries, and, from some superstitious motive, never worn except on occasions like the present, which called for more than an ordinary display of oriental grandeur. It could not, however, have been from poverty, or any scarcity of cloth among this people, as they are famous all over the Caucasus for their manufactures of wearing apparel.

The princess was merely distinguished from her youthful companions by the immense size of the scarlet saddle-cloth that covered her horse, the ends of which nearly reached the ground. It was showily decorated with gold embroidery, and

appeared quite as much entitled to be respected
for its age as the mantles and the hats.

A noble rode on each side of the horse of his
mistress, to take especial care that it did not shy
or make any false step which might endanger the
life of its precious burden. It was, however, a
very unnecessary precaution, and probably was
part of the ceremonial observed on these occasions, for not one of the noble knights who attended her sat firmer in the saddle than the fair
princess herself.

Several of the male attendants, of inferior rank,
in addition to the usual weapons worn by the
mountaineers, were armed with hatchets, for the
purpose of cutting down the brushwood that
might impede the progress of the cortège, and for
making rafts on which to transport the ladies and
their baggage across the rivers, should it be found
necessary.

In the midst of all this grandeur and assump-
tion of state, it was not a little ludicrous to see
the stock of provisions, composed of barley and
other meal, in bags, bottles of the skhou, and
shoulders and legs of mutton, dangling from their
saddle-bows.

The princess and her principal women wore large transparent white veils, which did not appear altogether destined to conceal their pretty features from observation, as, with the exception of one or two, the faces of all were in great part uncovered. It might be that only the old, or those not handsome, availed themselves of the shade of the muslin, for the others were really extremely beautiful, especially the princess, whose noble mien, and animated, commanding features, realized all we can imagine of an Amazon of old. The expression of her countenance was very different from that feminine gentleness which distinguishes the beauties of our own country, being rather the eye and character of one who could rule a kingdom, command an army, or set the world in a blaze.

I could not sufficiently admire the courteous bearing of the fine youth who had been delegated by his brother to conduct his bride to her future home. He leaped from his horse, and, after respectfully saluting her, in a manner that would have done honour to any one of the most gallant knights of the middle ages, drew his sword, and proceeded to make a long, and I dare say eloquent, oration ; but, as it underwent a double translation, I have no doubt its force and spirit were proportionably injured. He commenced by praising her beauty, comparing her eyes to diamonds, her cheeks to the roses of Arianoi (Persia), and her form to the graceful antelope.

Neither did he forget to eulogize the virtues and bravery of the bridegroom, his brother,—the number of enemies he had slain in battle, the courage of the bands of warlike clansmen who called him lord, the fertility of the country she was about to adopt as her own, and the vast flocks and herds of which she was to become the sole mistress. Then, turning the point of his sword alternately to the four quarters of the globe, swore he would protect her safely till he could deliver her to his brother, even at the sacrifice of his life and of the lives of his escort, should it become necessary—a declaration responded to by the whole band with loud acclamations.

The scene was altogether so romantic and novel in these prosaic matter-of-fact days, that I could scarcely bring myself to the belief of its reality. It appeared the more extraordinary as, notwithstanding the wild, warlike, roving manner of living pursued by this singular people, the deportment of all present exhibited a courteous-ness and urbanity that would have been admired in the most polished circles of civilized society.

Indeed, no actors, however talented, could give a representation half so correct or vivid of what we are led to believe were the manners of the feudal knights in the bygone days of chivalry. There was no straining after effect, no departure from nature, no attempt to caricature passion to the verge of absurdity. The courtesy manifested in their behaviour towards each other was the off-spring of kindness; the lively expression in their animated countenances emanated from real feeling; and their passionate eloquence spoke the language, not of premeditated, artificial compliment, but of sincerity. Their proffers of protection were not empty sounds, but made with a truthfulness of manner which carried conviction of their freedom from dissimulation; at the same time, the romantic character of the surrounding country in no way detracted from the singular picturesqueness of the scene.

There was the snow-clad mountain, the dark-grey jutting rock, the hollow abyss, the fertile valley, with its rushing torrent, the majestic forest trees, clothed in all their beautiful tints of autumn; nor must we forget the tiny cot of the mountain shepherd, surrounded by his flocks and herds ; the whole of which contrasted admirably with the groups of warriors and Amazons, mounted on their prancing steeds. Here we saw glittering the steel helmet of some sun-burnt warrior ; there the gaudy head-dress of a fair damsel, blooming with the rosy hue of health ; in one place, a casque of shining brass,—in another, a cap of the finest black Astrachan fur. These, together with the swarthy peasant in his sheep-skin turban, completed a picture, and produced an effect, which an imaginative painter might conceive, but which no language could describe.

CHAPTER XXVI.

Sketch of the Karatchai tribes—Origin of their name—Russian artifice — Successful stratagem — Ancient city of Madshar—Origin of its name—Ruins—Indifference of the Russian government to the remains of antiquity—Wanton demolition of Madshar—Opinions of Russian travellers respecting it—The Karatchai—Their religion—Character—Customs—Manners.

As the Karatchai tribes are among the most interesting and remarkable of those inhabiting the Caucasus, perhaps a few particulars respecting them may be acceptable to my readers, more especially as their history is not very generally known, and as some writers of the middle ages, and also others of more modern date, have attempted to prove that they and the Hungarians are descended from one common origin.

Although they speak a dialect of the Tartar language, and are considered to be of that race, a people by no means famous for personal beauty, the Karatchai tribes are among the handsomest inhabitants of the Caucasus, more resembling the Circassians in their fine forms, fair complexions, full dark eyes, and regular features, than any tribe not claiming that descent. In fact, they are denominated by the other Tartar tribes, Kara-Tcherkess (Black Circassians) ; not, however, that this appellation has been derived from their complexion, but from the country they inhabit, which lies partly on the banks of the Kara-ssu, or Kara-chai, (Black River,)—these people, like many others of the Caucasian tribes, borrowing from, or giving their name to, some river in their vicinity.

The Circassian knights do not acknowledge any affinity with the Karatchai, distinguishing them from the other Tartar tribes only as Kar-shaga-Kuscha (Tartar mountaineers). From the contiguity of their country to the great military road, Wladi-Kaukas, they have been repeatedly visited by Russian agents ; of these, M. Klaproth has given a more circumstantial account of their manners and customs than any other. From him we learn that they inhabit the Mingi-tau, a country lying at the base of the Elberous, towards the north, watered by the Upper Kouban, Kara-chai, Teberde, and other insignificant streams.

The character of the country inhabited by the Karatchai is mountainous, abounding with defiles, and on every side difficult of access. This circumstance was, in 1829, laid hold of by Russia as a pretence for requesting from the Circassian chiefs of the Western Caucasus permission for an army to pass through their possessions, from the Lower Kouban to Karatchai, for the purpose of chastising its inhabitants, who, it appeared, had given that power some real or ideal cause of umbrage.

That Russia might have complained with justice of the marauding disposition of the Karatchai we will admit; but from all I have been able to learn, and especially from subsequent events, that was not the principal object of the expedition. The Circassian chiefs, in their confiding simplicity, influenced no doubt by a plentiful and judicious distribution of valuable presents, consented to the passage of the Russian troops through the very centre of their territories, from one extremity to the other. But dearly, very dearly, have they paid for the confidence they reposed in a power which promises only to deceive.

Russia having by this means acquired what she desired,—an accurate knowledge of the interior of the country, its passes and defiles, together with the strength and resources of its inhabitants,— now threw off the mask, and, from that fatal hour, war and bloodshed, violence and rapine, have desolated the Western Caucasus ; from that time, indeed, we may date the commencement of the execution of a long-matured plan for the subjugation of the whole of the Caucasus ; for however long Russia might have carried on a war with the Caucasian tribes, previous to 1829, it was for the most part confined to the two Kabardahs and those provinces bordering on the Caspian Sea, if we except the unimportant and frequent skirmishes which have taken place during the last fifty years between the Tchernemorsky Cossacks, established on the right bank, and the Circassian tribes inhabiting the left bank of the Lower Kouban. The successive struggles between Turkey and Russia for the mastery of the forts on the Circassian coast, and which always involved the neighbouring tribes in the quarrel, from their close intimacy and alliance with the Ottoman Porte, cannot be regarded as an invasion of the Circassian territory by Russia, when we remember that these forts, or rather commercial depôts, were erected by Turkey, in accordance with stipulated treaties entered into with the natives; an account of which we have already laid before our readers.

We will now resume our slight sketch of the manners and customs of the Karatchai tribes. According to Klaproth and other travellers who visited the north-eastern line of the Caucasus, it appears that this people were at one time numerous, powerful, and independent. Their princes, who were both intellectual and highly civilized, resided in Madshar, a city not less famous for its great extent than the splendour of its architecture, and which, we should presume, from the accounts of the Asiatic historians, was at the zenith of its prosperity about the commencement of the second century of the Hegira. Albafeda makes mention of it in his geography, written in 1321, under the name of Kummadsher, a compound of Kum and Madsher, that ancient city having been situated on the left bank of the river Kuma, the Udon of Ptolemy.

Since the gradual decrease of the waters of the Euxine and the Caspian seas, together with that of the whole of the rivers that empty their waters into them, the Kuma, which at one time was a river of some importance, and discharged itself into the Caspian Sea, is now so diminished in volume as to have become completely absorbed in the heaps of mobile sand and marshy lakes in the Caspian steppe, formerly called Kumistan, from the circumstance of having been watered by that river. In fact, it is only when the waves of the Caspian, raised by tempestuous winds, overspread its shores, and when the river itself is swollen by the melting of the snow on the Caucasian mountains, that the waters of both in the present day ever form a junction,—and this is a combination that very rarely occurs.

The name Madshar, in some of the Tartar dialects, means a stone building; and Kirch-Madshar, by which that city was known to the neighbouring Tartar nations, signifies literally a place of many buildings, and to judge from the accounts of Güldenstadt, who visited it in the year 1773, there cannot be a doubt that it was at one time a splendid city, and even then contained upwards of thirty buildings, in tolerable preservation. Gmelin, one of the earliest Russian travellers in the Caucasus, was so enraptured with the ruins and buildings he then witnessed, that he calls it the "remains of a magnificent Scythian city."

But owing to the carelessness evinced by the

Russian government as to their preservation, or
a determination to destroy every vestige of antiquity in its dominions, a practice to which I
have before alluded when travelling in the Crimea
and elsewhere, this city, with its very interesting
remains, has entirely disappeared from the face
of the earth. Even the German, Von Klaproth, though a Russian agent, and consequently
guarded in his expressions, on witnessing this
wanton demolition of an object of so much curiosity to the antiquarian, and value to the historian,
as being the only ruins of a city in the Caucasus,
could not refrain from expressing his indignation.
He ascribes its total destruction to Count Paul
Potemkin, whose character was notorious for in-
famy, even in such a court as that of Catherine II.
This Russian Vandal, when governor of the provinces on the Caspian Sea, caused the whole of
the buildings then standing to be pulled down,
for the purpose of erecting the town and fortress of Ekaterinograd, although the surrounding country abounded with the finest stone for
building.

Hence we must now seek for the interesting
monumental inscriptions and various other valuable relics of antiquity in the walls of the new

town and fort, where, mutilated and defaced, they
remain to tell that civilized savages are of all
savages the worst! Even the foundation of the
old city can now with difficulty be recognised,
and, were it not for the mosaic pavement, the
coloured tiles and bricks, the European and
Asiatic coins, the bronze domestic utensils, gold
and silver trinkets, and other objects, indicating
that civilized man had once here an abiding
place, we might deem the whole of the vast site
where Madshar stood to have been a cemetery,
so numerous are the fragments of stones with
inscriptions that cover it. Indeed, this was the
view Professor Pallas, a good botanist and mineralogist, but not a very observant traveller, took of
Madshar when he visited it, and who, in a long
rambling account, gives us a description of this
ideal cemetery; assuredly he never could have
consulted any of the Tartar or eastern chronicles
upon this part of the Caucasus, or have perused
even any of the mutilated inscriptions that once
adorned the public buildings and gates of the
ancient city, or he never could have come to so
absurd a conclusion. Or did he purposely furnish this account, or the censor enforce it upon
him, for the purpose of concealing the Vandal

conduct of the Russian governor? If so, such are
the consequences of writing and publishing under
the control of a despotic government.

" Upon close investigation of these ruins," says
Pallas, (the Russian agent in the Caucasus,) " of
which scarcely a trace now exists, it appears to
have been a famous cemetery."

This was very different from the account of the
shrewd Klaproth, who visited Madshar during the
more liberal reign of the mild Alexander; that
intelligent traveller confirms beyond a doubt the
fact that Madshar was a great Tartar city, and
inhabited by a rich and a civilized people,—facts
proved by the coins that fell into his hands,
struck under the reign of the Tartar monarchs,
who there resided, together with a variety of information gleaned from perusing the inscriptions,
and other sources. To which I may add the details I received respecting that interesting city
from an intelligent German officer in the service
of Russia, and who had resided for some time
with his regiment at Ekaterinograd, in the immediate vicinity of the ruins.

Klaproth, when describing the descendants of
the ancient inhabitants of Madshar, the Karatchai,
says, that they not " only resemble the Circas-

sians in their form and features, but in many of their customs and manners. They are, however, not so much addicted to the practice of plundering the neighbouring tribes as that people, the word theft being seldom heard among them. They are also more industrious, subsisting chiefly by agriculture, and the profits arising from the sale of their manufactures, consisting of cloth (schal), felt (küss) for tents and carpeting, mantles (yamatschep), gunpowder, and various other articles of high value in the Caucasus.

" The religious tenets of the Karatchai formerly differed little from those of the other Tartar tribes in their vicinity. They worshipped the great spirit under the name of Tagris, and also the prophet Elijah, who they called Nebi Ilia, and believed frequently appeared on the summits of the high mountains, and to whom they were accustomed to offer sacrifices of lambs, milk, butter, cheese, and other fruits of the plenty with which heaven had blessed them. They are now, however, strict Mahometans, having been converted to Islamism by the famous Turkish missionary, Isaak Effendi, in 1782.

" The Karatchai bear a high character for morality; their children are educated with great care, and a strict regard to the principles of virtue. When a son is disobedient to his parents, and does not reform his conduct after being repeatedly admonished, he is compelled to stand at the door of the mosque, exposed to the view of the whole of the inhabitants of the village, when he is again solemnly exhorted to repent of the evil he has done, change his mode of living, and thus avert the guilt of bringing down the gray hairs of his parents with sorrow to the grave.

" Should this reproof be ineffectual, he is supplied with a few necessary articles, and commanded to quit the paternal roof, the door of which is now closed against him for ever, and he and his descendants remain aliens to the family.

" Deceit and treachery, so often the bane of civilized life, are to them nearly unknown; and should any native offend in this respect, or the stranger, who has come among them under the mask of friendship, be detected as a spy, the whole tribe fly to arms, and the delinquent atones for his falsehood with his life.

" Many of their customs are singular : the man who violates an agreement he has entered into forfeits ten sheep, or their value, to the inhabitants of the village or hamlet in which he resides. The ceremonial usually observed in taking an oath is, for the person to place his hand on the Koran, and invoke the Almighty to witness the truth of his declaration, which is always inviolably kept; and they as religiously obey the injunctions of the prophet not to omit daily prayers, or the annual fasts enjoined by the Mahometan religion.

" In temper they are warm and hasty, being excited to anger even by the most trifling cause; but if impetuous and irascible, they are at the same time easily appeased, and frankly acknowledge an error; nor are their manners less deserving commendation, for they are polite and mild, exceeding in this particular every other tribe in the Caucasus. To their rulers, the Circassian princes, they pay the most implicit respect and obedience, and are so charitable to their poorer brethren, that no member, whose conduct is deserving of esteem, can be said to want, as he is provided with all the common necessaries of life at the general expense of the tribe.

The soil of the country is fertile, producing abundance of corn, but, being cold and mountainous, yields no wine, for which they have an excellent substitute, *ssra* (beer), the best in the Caucasus, and somewhat resembling English porter. Like all the Caucasians, and indeed most eastern people, they are very partial to smoking. The tobacco they cultivate themselves, and after keeping a sufficient quantity for their own use, dispose of the remainder to their neighbours, which from its peculiar excellence and flavour is in high request.

" Their houses, built of fir, are mere huts in appearance, consisting of two rooms, and frequently only of one ; but the cleanliness visible throughout the little mansions, and the fireplace in the middle of the chamber, surrounded by bright copper cooking utensils, give them an air of comfort.

" The attire of the women, when out of doors, consists of woollen cloth trimmed with fur, and in summer usually of white cotton. The head-dress of the young girls is a cap of silver tissue, worn over their long plaited tresses, which, like those of the Circassians, frequently descend to the waist; while that of the married women, and of those more advanced in life, is a white muslin shawl.

" The dress of the men is, in many respects, like that of the Circassians; their weapons are also similar, except that a Karatchai never leaves home without a hunting spear, in consequence of the country being infested with bears of a prodigious size and strength, while wolves and wild cats are still more abundant, and panthers are not unfrequently met with. In short, game of every description is plentiful, and their hunting excursions often prove profitable, as they dispose of their furs to the Jews and Armenian pedlars, and often to the Russians on the Wladi-Kaukas line, to great advantage."

Whether the ancient city of Madshar was originally inhabited by the ancestors of the Magyars, of Hungary, from which they are said to derive their name, is a point which has been long contested by writers. Without pretending to give an opinion, this hypothesis is by no means improbable,—history affording sufficient evidence that the Hungarians are of eastern origin, and we know that they speak a dialect of the Arabic, like the Turks, Tartars, and other eastern nations.

CHAPTER XXVII.

Excursion in the interior—A bivouac in the mountains—
Alpine scenery — Animals — Chamois — Wild goats —
Wild sheep—Valuable qualities of their fleeces—Singu-
lar Caucasian bird, the Tschumuruk.

In the valley of the Phandra we parted from the
Karatchai princess and her escort; from whence
commenced the most difficult and fatiguing route
over which we had travelled in the Caucasus, as
our journey, for two days, lay over rugged mountains and deep glens, inaccessible to every crea-
ture save only the Circassian horse, or some wild
tenant of the woods. The aspect of the country,
although picturesque, was stern almost to savage-
ness, and, with the exception of a few mountain
huts, entirely desolate,—the inhabitants, with
their flocks and herds, having already retired to
some sheltered nook on the banks of their rivulets, to pass the dreary winter.

We were also exposed to the cold winds of the snowy mountains that towered far above us; and we had no other refuge by night from the keen blasts that howled around us, than the deserted chalet of some mountain shepherd, only used by him during the summer months.

Here was no chief to receive as at his hospitable board, no bard to greet us with his song of welcome : we were completely abandoned to our own resources ; but a people like the Circassians, so accustomed to a wandering life, find themselves at home in the most inhospitable desert, if they can but meet with water, and wood for fuel, which fortunately abound throughout the Caucasus.

When we made a halt for the night, the first thing done was to unsaddle the horses, and lead them to some fertile spot, where they could find pasturage and water,—these people, like true cavaliers, always providing for the wants of their horses before attending to themselves. A fire is next lighted, the saddle-cloth spread for a carpet to sit upon, the saddle placed for a pillow; then, enveloped in the ample folds of the tchaouka, they resign themselves, after performing their usual evening avocations, to the enjoyment of their favourite tchibouque; first, however, the evening meal must be prepared, the only one in which these people may be said to indulge. The preparation of this meal is performed in turn, and to it each individual contributes his stock of provisions, or, as was the case at present, our expedition across the mountains was accompanied by a few sumpter horses, loaded with such provisions as might be found necessary, independent of the game furnished by our guns while travelling.

First of all, a cup of coffee (an article now somewhat scarce in the Caucasus) is prepared, as an accompaniment to the pipe, while the supper is cooking, which generally consists of hot barley-cakes, the savoury *tschicklikha*, composed of minced mutton, rice, &c.—a dish similar to the pilaff; these are succeeded by honey and dried fruits, by way of dessert, varied, perhaps, by a few hard-boiled eggs; and, last of all, the refreshing skhou, to slake the thirst. Let him but have these, and a mountaineer of the Caucasus asks no more; neither will a European be inclined to despise them, for the mutton of these countries is not surpassed by any other in delicacy of flavour; and should the rifle have brought down a fat buck, a pheasant, or a wild turkey, the eastern ragout is, we may be assured, not the worse for the addition.

The other articles are also excellent of their kind, and the cooking perfectly agreeable to our palate.

I must not forget to mention, that this vigilant people never resign themselves to rest or repose without stationing a sentinel,—a precaution rendered necessary, not only by the unsettled state of the country, but by the numerous wild animals that haunt the forests; and none pay more attention to their weapons of defence: these, under whatever circumstances a Circassian may be placed, he cleans regularly every night; and we may assert, that in no arsenal do we find arms kept in higher order. These, of course, are part of the evening's occupations where he halts for the night. The guns and pistols are then primed and loaded, and, together with the sabre, are placed by the pillow,—but he never parts with the poniard, asleep or awake. Having concluded his avocations, a short prayer is offered up to the Giver of all good, and he then resigns himself to sleep.

Supposing the night passed, and the necessary

preparations made previous to starting, we will resume our route. At one time we wound our way round the base of a tremendous cliff, crowned by an avalanche that appeared ready to crush us every moment; at another, hung over a yawning precipice of such fearful depth that, an unlucky step, and both horse and rider would sleep in eternity. In one place, torrents poured down the rocks in foaming cascades; and then, perhaps, some clear tranquil stream swept round the base of a mountain, in a majestic curve, fertilizing the land over which it ran. Here, were bare pyramidal rocks, jutting up among trees of gigantic growth, principally the oak, beech, and linden; there, columnar masses of red basaltic porphyry, mingling with wild apple-trees, walnut, and other fruit trees,—altogether presenting a truly romantic spectacle.

The inhabitants of this alpine desert were such as we only find amidst scenery of this description: the mountain-raven, with its blood-red bill and scarlet legs, disturbed in its solitary nest, flew over our heads, croaking its doleful note; the eagle, monarch of this dreary region, soared still higher to seek some retreat uninvaded by the footsteps of dreaded man; and the gigantic vulture, securely perched on the peak of a lofty crag, boldly looked down as we passed; while the growling of the bear, the hideous screaming of the jackal, and the howl of the wolf, repeatedly fell on our ears from the dense forests around us; at the same time, the chamois and wild-goats bounded from pinnacle to pinnacle whose altitude was so great that the animals appeared like so many squirrels.

Of these goats there are two kinds, very common in this part of the Caucasus. The one is the well-known ibex, and the other, which roves about in herds, is a splendid animal, somewhat resembling the goat of Europe in shape, but much larger, and with limbs as slender as those of a deer, and long curved horns. Their flesh is not more esteemed by the mountaineers than their skins, which, on account of the fine long hair, are always used by some of the tribes as carpets when kneeling in prayer, being connected with a superstitious idea that their prayers will then be responded to by the Great Spirit.

All our attempts to get a shot at these wary animals proved ineffectual; the slightest rustle of our horses through the brushwood, nay, our distant approach, sufficed to send whole troops to the summit of some inaccessible cliff. Hence

the Circassians find these, of all the wild animals
in their mountains, the most difficult to entrap ;
for, in addition to the quickness of their eyesight
and hearing, their smell is perhaps unequalled by
that of any other animal ; and as they never graze
or sleep without turning their face to the wind,
they are enabled to discern an enemy even at a
great distance.

These interesting animals—called by the natives, Turi, and by the Circassians, Tschickzwi—
establish among themselves a community, which
displays an intelligence in its regulations perfectly surprising : for instance, when grazing, they
station sentinels, whose watchfulness guards the
safety of their comrades by apprising them of the
approach of danger. During their rambles they
always follow a leader, as distinguished for his
boldness as his great size ; and such is their confidence in his sagacity, that, were he to jump
down a precipice, the whole of his companions
would not hesitate to do the same ; indeed, this
is sometimes the case when hard pressed by the
hunter, or pursued by wild animals, which,
obliging them to take some tremendous leap, the
young and weakly, unable to accomplish the feat,
fall victims to the daring temerity of their leader.

The colour of their very fine hair is not uniformly the same, though a sort of grey-white, or perhaps a stone colour, predominates.

In addition to these animals, the mountaineers informed me that wild sheep, of a smaller size and more agile than the domestic breed, are sometimes found in the neighbouring mountains, in which the Kara-ssu, the Tscherek-jana, the Teberde, Rion, Kouban, Inguri, Tscheness-tzquali (the Hippus of the ancients), and other Caucasian rivers, have their source. But these districts being inhabited by the Karatchai, the Balkhars, Ghigni, or Tchegims, the Urus-Kuscha, and other Tartar tribes, who, it appears, are very industrious manufacturers of cloth, they have nearly destroyed these interesting animals, for the sake of their fine wool, which, if we may credit their accounts, preserves its natural colour—a fine bright yellow, or sometimes black—in defiance of the influence of time, or of exposure to the weather. Such, then, being the valuable qualities of the fleece, we cannot wonder that animals affording so considerable a source of profit should become nearly extinct. It may be interesting to future travellers, and to the curious, to ascertain whether these sheep may not be a remnant of

those described by the ancient Roman and Greek
writers as belonging to the barbarous tribes of
the Caucasus in their day.

Notwithstanding the various inquiries I made
with this view, I was unable to establish the existence of that singular bird described by Pallas
as inhabiting the south side of the mountains I
had been now traversing. According to his account, it is a species of pheasant, but much
larger, called by the Karatchai and Balkhar Tartars, Tschumuruk, with five talons on each foot,
and a plumage beautifully variegated. It is said to
frequent the haunts of the turi (goats), for whom
it serves as a guard by its peculiar whistle, which
warns them of the approach of the murderous
huntsman. As this bird, according to report, is
endued with such extraordinary powers, it is a
pity that nature did not appoint it as the guardian
of the timid and interesting race of sheep we have
just described!

One singular coincidence, in reference to the
Urus-Kuscha tribe, alluded to above, I cannot
forbear mentioning. It appears that the name
by which they are known to the Circassians is
the same as the appellation by which they distinguish the Russians—Urus (Russian), Kuscha

(Tartar.) They are also said to resemble the peasants of Old Russia in their personal appearance,
particularly in having, like them, red beards and
light hair, and to be some of the most ancient inhabitants of the Caucasus; but whether their
lauguage is a dialect of that spoken by the Muscovites, I have not been able to ascertain; neither
can I explain their affinity to the Tartars, though
we must presume them, on account of their name,
to be of that origin.

CHAPTER XXVIII.

Ascent of the Tschuman-tau—Splendid scenery—Luxuriant
vegetation—Botanical plants—Minerals—Anecdote of
the Emperor Paul and a Russian mineralogist—Gold
mines in the Caucasus — Perilous excursion — Arrival
among the Suoni tribes—Natural strength of the country they inhabit—The Porta Cumana—Opinions respecting its situation.

We continued our journey, over a country
similar to that I have just described, till at length
we came to the Tschuman-tau, one of the
highest mountains connected with the Elberous
chain; but owing to the snow, which had already
covered the summit, we were obliged to deviate
from the beaten track, and wind around its south-
eastern side, even my hardy fellow travellers
not deeming it prudent to attempt the ascent at
this season of the year.

Upon reaching our highest elevation, what a
prospect unfolded itself to view! and the fine

weather with which we had been favoured during
the last ten days enabled us to enjoy it in perfection.   On one side lay the Euxine, smooth and
bright as a sheet of glass ; the plains of Mingrelia,
covered with interminable forests ; and the rising
hills of Imeritia, which, from the great height we
had attained, appeared like so many mole hillocks.
On the other, rose, besides the magnificent Elberous, with its double peak, which, towering high
above all, appeared to command the whole chain,
the craggy summits of four or five other splendid
alps, together with the vast heights over which
we had travelled the last few days, shelving down
to the Euxine.   Here we encamped about an
hour, for the purpose of resting our weary
horses, and preparing the noon-day meal,—which
permitted me to examine the beautiful plants
and flowers that bloomed in this favoured land ;
for, however high the ascent, we see luxuriant
vegetation mingling even with the snow of centuries : there was the centaurea montana, the
gentiana cruciata and sèptemfida, the tall sca-
biosa and amarella, the campanula and rhamnus
lycioides, with pinks of every species, and hundreds of wild roses of every colour, intermingled
with the beautiful azalea pontica, the rhododen-

dron caucasicum and common rhododendron, the morus tatarica, and various other stunted shrubs, all interesting to the botanist, and agreeable to the lovers of the picturesque, as, extending their branches and tendrils from one to the other, they covered the whole side of the mountain like a carpet, and spread their aromatic fragrance far and wide.

From the little geological research I was able to make, for my escort never halted for any length of time, except at night, I should be inclined to think, owing to the frequent occurrence of calcarious spars, compact and porous, the milk quartz, and other substances and indications, particularly the pebbles and mineral particles found in the brooks and rivulets, that various kinds of ore abound in these mountains; indeed, the iron, saltpetre, sulphur, and lead, here obtained, are even now made use of by the natives; the latter is so plentiful, that one of the mountains in this part of the Caucasus is called Isdi-chong (lead hill) by the Tartars, and Kuscha-tau (lead mountain) by the Circassians; and, judging from the strata on the rugged banks of the rivers, it may be inferred without doubt that coal is plentiful.

As for gold, silver, and precious stones, I was
not so fortunate as to find any, although I travelled in that part of the Caucasus where the
ancients tell us the brooks were so full of gold
that the natives were accustomed to catch it by
means of fleeces.

Various attempts have been made by Russia to
discover and obtain possession of the rich mines
supposed to exist in this part of the Caucasus,
hitherto without success. During the reign of the
Emperor Paul, an exploring Russian mineralogist,
having found a vast rock abounding with *cat gold*,
concluded that he had at length met with the
treasure, hastened to St. Petersburg to communicate the welcome intelligence to the emperor;
that mad monarch instantly dispatched Count
Musin Puschkin the inspector of mines, with a
whole army of miners to take possession of this
inexhaustible supply of gold, which it was supposed would furnish sufficient to pave the streets
of the capital. But, alas! mineralogist, inspector,
and monarch, were doomed to be disappointed,
and to experience the truth of the old proverb,
" All is not gold that glitters."

Still the hope of finding the gold mines of the
Caucasus, so frequently alluded to by ancient

writers, is not abandoned by the Russian government; indeed, there is scarcely an intelligent Russian we meet with who does not feel confident that these mines will one day prove the source of inexhaustible wealth to the autocrat. In consequence of this expectation, if the information I received be correct, many an intelligent foreigner, tempted by the prospect of acquiring immense wealth, having been furnished with an escort, assistants, and every other necessary required for a mining expedition, has journeyed to the Caucasus, but never returned, falling a victim in all probability to the hostility of the Circassians.

This would also have been the fate, if his destiny had not befriended him, of the German botanist and mineralogist, M——, who visited that part of this chain of mountains on the coast near the fort of Bombora, during the early part of the summer of 1836. Although he had no intention more warlike, no object more hostile, than to procure a few specimens of minerals and flowers, and was attended by a strong guard of armed Cossacks, it was enough that he was Russian; consequently, the greater number of his escort fell by the bullets of the mountaineers, and his own escape was little short of a miracle. Yet he was under the protection of the chief of the district, Scharavaschedze; but the influence of that recreant Abasian ended when his alliance with Russia began, and he is now an outlaw, branded as a traitor by his countrymen, and deserted by nearly the whole of his clansmen, who have obliged him to seek refuge from their poniards under the shelter of the Russian cannon at Bombora.

We experienced much greater difficulty, and encountered far more peril, in descending the Tschuman-tau than in the ascent, for, having followed the serpentine windings of a small torrent that roared in a deep abyss, we came at least every quarter of an hour to some projecting crag, partly clothed with brushwood, their roots affording the only security for the footsteps of ourselves and horses. Riding was entirely out of the question, and so tedious was our excursion, that we did not arrive at our destination, a small village belonging to the Suoni tribes, in the glen beneath, till the shades of night had obscured the whole horizon; and if we had not been so fortunate as to attract a mountain shepherd to our aid, who conducted us by a more circuitous but less perilous path, we should have been obliged to bivouac in some sheltered nook for the night.

Such is the character of many parts of the interior of this country, not affording even safe footing to perhaps the most intrepid people that ever dashed across a plain, or bounded over a mountain. In the present instance, had we undertaken this excursion in rainy weather, the lives of every one of the party, had we attempted to advance, might have fallen a sacrifice; and though I have often experienced many a rough specimen of mountain travelling in some of the most inaccessible districts of Europe and America, I confess I was heartily glad when we arrived at the door of a worthy elder, where we passed the night, finding, as usual, a hospitable board and a comfortable divan on which to repose our weary frames.

The tribe among whom we had now taken up our quarters, called by the Circassians Suoni, by the Tartars, Ebse, and by the Georgians, Svanetti, is also included in the confederacy of the Circassian knights, and may be considered as one of the most numerous and powerful in this part of the Caucasus, occupying the whole of the mountains that extend from the base of the Elberous to the

frontiers of Imeritia and Mingrelia, and are thus
constituted by nature the guardians of Circassia
against any attack with which they may be menaced
by the Russian armies in Georgia or Mingrelia.

Like the Abasians, we may rank them among
the most ancient inhabitants of the Caucasus,
having been mentioned by the earliest writers.
It appears that they have never been subdued,
for the influence the Circassian knights exercise over them (several of whom reside in this
province) arises more from the respect paid to
their heroism, and the necessity they feel of
unanimity, than from any recognition of their
authority.

If we may judge from the great natural strength
of the country inhabited by the Suoni tribes, its
conquest would be an absolute impossibility, intersected as it is in every direction by steep rugged
passes and dangerous defiles, these being flanked
by lofty rocks, and overgrown with brushwood,
where it is only necessary that a few resolute men
should post themselves, in order to be able to
annihilate an army ; and that these passes might
be rendered still more formidable as a defence,
the entrances to several of them are fortified with
stone walls, of such antiquity, that we must

believe them to have been erected at some very remote period.

The Suoni in their persons are both athletic and robust, and none of the tribes among whom I mingled are more healthy-looking ; and perhaps none preserve a stronger bond of union, or are more exempt from intestine feuds. The situation of their mountains, bordering on Imeritia and Mingrelia, and their own numerical weakness, for they are not able to muster more than from three to four thousand fighting men, have taught them the necessity of union. In consequence of this, they boast, that while other parts of the Caucasus have suffered, time after time, from foreign invasion, and have been thrown into anarchy, arising from petty feuds and jealousies, they have continued to cultivate their fields in peace, and tend their flocks and herds without fear or interruption.

Between the Tschuman-tau we had just traversed and the Elberous, with its chain of alps, lies a strong defile, which connects Mingrelia and Imeritia with the whole of the Western Caucasus on to the Kouban. This route we should have taken in preference to that along the coast to Mingrelia, were it not that the chiefs who accompanied

me were solicitous to communicate with the elders
of the tribes on the coast, with a view of strengthening their mutual alliance, and of making preparations for the ensuing campaign, and also that
we had hopes of finding a bark to convey me to
Turkey.

The entrance to this defile is said to have been
at one time fortified and defended by an iron gate,
from which extended a wall sixty leagues in length,
supposed to have been erected by Mirwan, King
of Georgia, who reigned over these countries a
century before the Christian era. But it appears
not a single vestige of this wall is now visible;
the Circassians, however, would certainly not
trouble themselves about any such matter, and as
the whole country on the frontiers of Mingrelia
and Imeritia is thickly covered with very high
brushwood, the future research of some exploring antiquary may perhaps discover indications of its having existed.

Moreover, some learned Turks and Persians
inform us, that the entrance to this valley was
actually that described by Pliny, where the famous
Caucasian gate was erected, so celebrated among
the ancients.

For, says that learned historian, " in the country of the Diduri and Ssodi," probably the Suoni, "is the Caucasian gate, a prodigious work of nature, being rocks of gigantic elevation, closed in with an iron gate, under which runs the Diri-odoris. On one side of this ponderous gate, perched upon a rock, stands a castle, called Kumania, so strongly fortified as to be capable of withstanding the passage of a numerous army."

Reineggs, one of the earliest Russian travellers in the Caucasus, maintains that this defile is indeed that mentioned by Pliny; but as travellers (and many reviewers) seldom agree, at least when theories are in question, Klaproth boldly refutes this supposition, and asserts that his defile, formed by the Tcherek, is absolutely that described by Pliny, as it completely intersects the whole northern part of the Caucasus to Dariela, on the frontiers of Georgia, where, he says, are still to be seen the ruins of the ancient castle of Dariela,* which he concludes to be the Kumania of the ancients.

Without offering a positive opinion, Klaproth

---

* This interesting relic of antiquity was entirely destroyed by the Russians, during the time they were engaged in constructing their great military road, the Wladi-Kaukas.

in all probability is right in his conjecture, as the pass he alludes to corresponds in a greater number of features with that described by the ancients than the defile mentioned by Reineggs. Still a great stumbling block exists, which Klaproth has not been able to explain away. What affinity exists between the words Tcherek and Diri-odoris? for the names of great rivers are seldom so entirely altered as to leave no trace of the original in any language whatever; but when we consider the inhabitants of the Caucasus, a people so unsettled, so accustomed to rove from place to place, and to call their villages, rivers &c. after the name of some lamented warrior, in all probability the Diri-odoris has been transformed to Tcherek, the name of some victorious chief.

Reineggs, when talking of his defile, says, " It must be manifest to every traveller that the Porta Cumana on the south side was opened by human labour, and that this prodigious valley was formed by the excavation of miners; and probably the rich galleries and shafts are only choked with earth, so as not to be discoverable." According to his opinion, it was from this pass the ancients derived their wonderful supply of gold! " For," continues he, " if we can depend upon ancient accounts, the ore in this valley was so abundant, so rich, so easily wrought, that a few men were sufficient to furnish the stated quantity of gold and silver."

Russian research has, however, been hitherto unsuccessful in finding the slightest trace of these extraordinary mines; but that gold exists in these mountains I think we may infer from the fact that this precious metal is frequently met with in the brooks and rivulets after heavy rains; and the Suoni to this day use sheep-skins in catching it.

COSTUME OF A SUONI CHIEF AND HIS FAMILY.

CHAPTER XXIX.

Traces of Amazons in the Caucasus, in the seventeenth century—Customs and manners of the Suoni tribes—Their religion—Habitations—Domestic animals—Natural productions of the country—Wild animals—Origin of the people—Some account of the tribes inhabiting the eastern division of the Caucasus—Nogay Tartars—Their extraordinary diminution—Attributed to the butcheries of the Cossack Suwarrow.

In addition to the interest attached to the mountains of which we are now treating as being those represented by the ancients as abounding with precious metals, we are led to believe, from the tradition of the Circassians, that they were at one time inhabited by Amazons. Indeed, the opinion that a race of warlike women resided in some part of the Caucasus appears to have been very general among the neighbouring nations, even so late as the early part of the seventeenth century, for Lamberti, a monk, who happened to be at this period in Mingrelia, states—

" During the time I was staying in Mingrelia, the prince of that country received intimation that numerous bands of warriors, in full armour, and well provided with all the materiel of war, had issued from the interior of the Caucasus, and were carrying fire and sword into the territories of the Muscovites, and also into the mountainous districts of the Svanetti (Suoni), and the Karatscholi (Karatchai), bordering upon his own territories.

" After a long and desperate struggle with the mountaineers, these adventurers were repulsed, when the greater number of the slain were discovered to be women, in the prime of life. Specimens of the armour of these Amazons having been presented to the Dadian, were found on examination to be unusually splendid, being composed of helmets, cuirasses, cuises, and gauntlets, made of the finest polished steel, and so ingeniously contrived as to be perfectly flexible to every part of the body. The cuirass, which reached to the waist, was lined with bright scarlet woollen stuff.

" Nor were their buskins, adorned with studs of shining brass, less generally admired; and even their arrows were executed with considerable labour and ingenuity, being full four spans in length, gilt, and barbed with the finest polished steel."

Such is the account of Signor Lamberti; but it is highly probable, after all, that these elegantly-equipped Amazons were really the wives and daughters of the Circassian knights, who, to this day, in cases of emergency, accompany the men to the field of battle. We may also be allowed to question the monk's account of the magnificence of their armour, or, at all events, to presume it is exaggerated, as so unusual an event as bands of female warriors carrying their arms into the heart of Muscovy would assuredly have become generally known in Europe.

The religion of the Suoni may be said to be a modification of Christianity, for they observe many of the fasts enjoined by the Greek church, and make a pilgrimage once or twice a-year to the ruins of some of their churches, or other holy shrines. An old man, of known sanctity, officiates as priest when his services are required, for which he is rewarded by each family, once a-year, with a fat sheep. When celebrating any of their festivals, such as Christmas, Easter, &c., they are most liberal in their hospitality, compelling every stranger, poor or rich, who may happen to be in their neighbourhood, to partake of their good cheer.

The Suoni speak a dialect of the Mingrelian, and in their dress also resemble that people, while their customs and manners differ little from those of the other Caucasian tribes already described. In hospitality and courtesy to strangers well recommended, and in respect to their elders and chiefs, they are not exceeded by any ; but woe to the traveller who might enter their settlements without some proof of the integrity of his intentions.

The only difference I observed in the culinary preparations was, a substitute for the almost universal pilaff, in the form of mutton broth, served in small earthen basins, after the meat was dis-

patched. Like the other Circassian tribes, they
are still ignorant that knives and forks form a
cleanlier and more convenient medium for con-
veying food to the mouth than the fingers.

It must be confessed, that when our whole
party were seated on their little carpets around
the huge smoking copper cauldron of one of these
patriarchal chiefs, devouring its contents with
their fingers—the lord of the entertainment at the
same time politely pointing out with his poniard
the most delicate morsels to his guests, etiquette
forbidding him to join the circle himself—they
formed a picture which might well astonish a re-
fined denizen of Europe. Yet, however fastidious
his taste may be, let him ride four or five hours,
without refreshment, over a mountainous country
like the Caucasus, and then find himself seated
near such a cauldron, filled with a savoury ragout, and I suspect his predilection for forks and
spoons would vanish before the pleadings of
hunger, and he would find the humble repast of the
mountaineers quite as palatable as the recherché
viands of the most accomplished cuisinier of the
day.

Instead of the wine and bosa so generally found
at the houses of the other tribes we had visited,

we were here, for the first time, plentifully re-
galed with beer, by no means to be despised. I
could not forbear remarking that these people,
notwithstanding salt is easily procured from their
neighbours, the Mingrelians, prefer using sour
milk as a substitute, which appears rather to con-
duce to their health than otherwise,—at least,
one thing is certain, that no peasants in any part
of Europe are more free than the inhabitants of
these provinces are in general from eruptive diseases, and, if we may judge from their appearance,
none are more healthy ; a fact attested by the great
age to which the inhabitants generally attain, and
the number of fine children that everywhere meet
the eye. This may perhaps be, in some measure,
attributed to the circumstance, that they consume
vast quantities of honey, and never indulge in
spirituous liquors ; to which we may add, that they
take a great deal of exercise in the open air.

The Suoni are not so neat in all that apper-
tains to domestic economy as the Circassians,
neither are their houses so commodious, being,
in fact, mere hovels, resembling those of the Tartars, which I described when travelling in Krim-
Tartary. The roofs are, in general, level with
the surface of the ground, and the little dwelling

itself lies burrowed in the side of a rock, on the banks of some running stream or spring.   In the centre of these huts is an opening intended for the purposes of admitting light and expelling smoke ; adjoining to these are the sheds for their cattle, and store-houses for preserving the produce of the field during winter,—all built in the same primitive manner.

These huts appear, however, suited to their wants, as they never remain stationary for any length of time.   In summer they wander from mountain to mountain with their flocks and herds, and during winter remain quietly on the fertile banks of some rivulet ; but, as they think it too much labour to manure their land, when it becomes exhausted by repeated crops they remove to another spot.   Hence, if we were not aware of this being the general practice of the people, and in a greater or less degree that of all the tribes of the Western Caucasus, we might be led to believe, from the frequent recurrence of ruined hamlets and homesteads, that the country had been recently laid waste by some invading army.

As may be supposed, the Suoni, from the nature of their country, are a people entirely pastoral in

their habits. At the same time that they derive
from their narrow dales sufficient corn for their
own consumption, they maintain numerous flocks
and herds. Their horses are small and rough-look-
ing, but very hardy, and none are better adapted
for mountain-travelling, owing to their sure-
footedness ; hence they derive considerable profit
by selling them to their neighbours, the Imeritians
and Mingrelians. They have also a good breed
of asses, and their mules are much in demand.

Every hamlet and homestead through which
we passed we found infested, like those of the
Krim Tartars with dogs of the wolf breed, whose
incessant clamour and pertinacious pursuit of a
stranger are extremely annoying. In addition to
this canine torment, they have a fine race of grey-
hounds, resembling those of the Circassians in
Lower Abasia, kept for coursing, an amusement
for which they entertain a strong attachment.

It would appear from the numerous ruins of
churches and other buildings, that the Suoni
were at one time more civilized than they are at
the present day ; still, being moderate in their
desires, and having abundance of cattle and corn
to supply their wants, together with every description of game, and at the same time protected

from invasion by the fastnesses of their mountains, we may term them a happy people.

The chiefs and elders of the Suoni, being allied with the Circassian knights by family ties,
are on the most friendly terms with them, and in
general with all their neighbours, who look up to
their mountains as a secure asylum in the event
of being expelled from their own country by aggression.   In their laws, customs, and manners,
they are perfectly patriarchal, living under the
jurisdiction of those among their elders whose
wisdom and influence entitle them to such a distinction.

The dales and sides of the mountains inhabited
by the Suoni are well covered with forest timber, including immense trees of that beautiful red
wood, the Taxus, together with oak and linden
of the most gigantic dimensions.   Here I found
the bark of that most useful tree, the linden,
again in high request, as these people manufacture from it their summer tents, which are
perfectly impervious to rain.   Lofty walnut trees
abound in favoured situations, where also the
vine and various kinds of fruit trees thrive with
no common luxuriance.

The system of agriculture pursued by these

people differs little from that of the other mountaineers before described, and their flocks and herds are also very similar. Their forests, however, being more inaccessible and savage, abound with prodigious quantities of game of every description, and also with wild animals, such as the bear, wolf, lynx, and wild cat; neither is the panther, which infests part of Imeritia and Georgia, any stranger to their valleys.

We have very little information that can be depended upon respecting the origin of this people; Suoni, in the Circassian dialect, merely indicating an inhabitant of the alps. They are only known to Russia by the name of Ssuanes, and as the greatest of all depredators upon her territory; and, from the inaccessible nature of the country, her troops have never been able to chastise them. In all probability they belong to the Lazi, or Laze, known to have been the same people as the Cholchians described by Procopius, and other ancient writers, and who at one time formed a powerful state, their territories extending from Lazestahn, near Trebizond, through Gourial, Mingrelia, Imeritia, and Georgia, on to the ancient Iberia; dialects of the language of the latter country are still spoken in the whole of these provinces ; and as the Suoni speak the same dialect, and resemble the Lazi* in features, &c., they are in all probability the same people.

Among the other great tribes of the Caucasus, to the north and north-east of the Suoni, inimical to the Russian government, and which continue to infest the great military road Wladi-Kaukas, we may enumerate the Ingushes, and their kindred tribes, the Tushi and Tschetschenzes, together with the Ossetinians, as the most considerable. The latter, although not quite so murderous in their hostile demonstrations as the others, are any thing but friendly towards their Russian neighbours.

To the south of these, and towards Georgia, the Gudamaquari, Chewsuri, Pschawi, and others, have never been subdued by Russia, and constantly communicate with the Circassian knights, aiding them with auxiliaries and other valuable assistance ; and it was for the purpose of holding

---

* The Lazi tribes have been repeatedly confounded with the Lesghians, nay, in many maps and geographical accounts they are described as such, whereas nothing can be more erroneous, the Lesghians, who derive their descent from the Saracens, not having the slightest affinity with the Lazi, either in language, feature, or form.

a conference with the chiefs of these tribes that my konak and his companions were now journeying.

With respect to the Ingushes, I had an opportunity of seeing a band of these mountain warriors, who had joined the camp of the confederated chiefs on the Ubin, and, to judge from their features, height, and other characteristics, they were certainly a very different race from every other I had seen in the Caucasus. They are short, thick-set, and very muscular, their great strength being equally serviceable to them in the use of the bow and the sabre; yet neither weapon, however dexterously they may use it, will ensure them victory when engaged in athletic or martial exercises against a Circassian or an Abasian, whose superior agility usually gives them the advantage.

Professor Güldenstadt, one of the most impartial and intelligent writers among the Russian agents that visited the north-eastern part of the Caucasus, and who had an opportunity of studying the national character and language of the Ingush tribes, seems to consider them as the most genuine race of Alans now existing, founding his

opinion upon several words in their peculiar dialect—such as *Dada* (father), &c.

The Ingushes designate themselves by the name
of Lamar, which has no other signification than
that of mountaineer; but of the time when they
first settled in the Caucasus, or of their origin,
they are totally ignorant. Every attempt made
by the Ottoman Porte—through the agency of
its clever missionary, Isaak Effendi, of such celebrity in the Caucasus — to convert them to
Islamism, failed, in the same manner as that of
the Russian government to win them over to em-
brace the tenets of the Greek church; and they
now profess the same creed as that of their ancestors from time immemorial,—perfectly simple,
as that of the other Caucasian tribes, (not professing Mahometanism,) being confined to the
worship of one only God, whom they denominate
Dada, Daal, Thaut.

Sunday is celebrated by them in the same manner as among Christians, so far as regards its observation as a day of rest, but public devotion is
altogether omitted, the day being usually passed
in amusement. Their weekly division of time,
in common with the other Caucasian tribes, also

corresponds with that of Christianity, which religion, there can be little doubt, they at some former period professed.

As a proof of this, we may mention, that a church still exists on the banks of the Assai, not far distant from the Upper Tcherek, of great antiquity, said to be an exact model of the holy sepulchre at Jerusalem. This church is regarded with the highest veneration, not only by the Ingushes, but by the whole of the neighbouring tribes, to whom it is the object of an annual pilgrimage; and, singular to say, it is still endowed with a revenue suited to the pastoral habits of the people, consisting of a certain number of heads of cattle, which are given by each tribe to the elders, and appropriated to the purpose of keeping it in repair, and supporting the devotee who might visit it from some distant province, or the criminal who should seek refuge in its walls.

So sacred, indeed, is the estimation in which this church is held in the Caucasus, that its name is invoked by several tribes as a confirmation of the most solemn oaths; and when viewing it at a distance, the natives bow their faces to the earth.*

---

* Both Pallas and Klaproth, who visited this church, mention the veneration expressed for it by the people; but

I observed among the Suoni tribe several
Nogay Tartars, so easily distinguished by their
Mogul features ; and on inquiring, I found that
several families of this people were settled among
them and the other mountaineers of Upper Abasia.
What an inconsiderable remnant of a once-power-
ful nation ! who, after the extinction of the empire of Ghenghis Khan, gave laws to the inhabitants of vast provinces in Europe and Asia ;
for, with the exception of those established on

they do not agree respecting the inscription over the principal entrance,—Pallas declaring it to be in the Latin language, and written in Gothic characters, while Klaproth
metamorphoses it into Georgian, or rather, he says, that
" this was the language in which the now illegible inscription was originally written." They both, however, assert
that it is built of hewn stones, having over the principal
entrance a few rude figures, carved in alto-relievo, repre-
senting a man sitting on a chair, and above him a hand
issuing out of the clouds, apparently in the act of presenting
him with a rule.   On either side of this is another figure,—
that on the left holds a cross in one hand, and a sword in
the other, while that on the right carries a bunch of grapes
suspended over his shoulder on a pole.   Klaproth says, that
the Ingushes still preserve a few apartments, which he pre-
sumes are those formerly occupied by the monks, filled with
relics, books, &c.; but no threat, bribery, or persuasion,
could prevail upon the guardians to allow a stranger to enter
them.

the Steppe Moloshnia Voda, near the sea of Azow, and whom I described in my late work when speaking of Krim-Tartary, they may be said to be almost extinct, and entirely so as a nation.

If we consult history, we shall find the Nogay Tartars at no very distant date governing in Astrakan, and disputing with great bravery its conquest by Russia; and even so recently as the period when Catharine II. seized the throne of Krim Tartary, they occupied with their numerous flocks and herds, not only the vast steppe from the Kouban to the Don, but nearly the whole of the immense district of Kumestan, or the Caspian Steppe; and as an evidence of the spirit by which they were actuated, and of a confidence in their strength, they exhibited in the year 1780 such manifestations of insurrectionary feeling, that Suwarrow and his legions were sent to reduce them to obedience.

This monster, the wholesale butcher of the Poles, must either have dispersed them to the four quarters of the vast empire of Russia, or slaughtered them without regard to age or sex, for from that time to the present day, so insignificant has been the miserable remnant, that they are never mentioned in Russia, except as a degraded horde, composed of a few dozen families, only remarkable for their indigence and want of courage, the veriest poltroons and slaves.

END OF VOL. I.

T. C. Savill, Printer, St. Martin's Lane, Charing Cross.

Printed in Great Britain
by Amazon